EXPLORING DEEP SPACE AND BEYOND

CINEMAKER PRESS

This book is distributed in Canada by Starstruck North Productions. For information please call (416)513-6606 or write to 3555 Don Mills Road, Suite 6166, Toronto Ontario M2H 3N3

First Printing, First Edition: February 1993
Published in the United States of America

ISBN#0-9627508-7-5

AN INTRODUCTION

Science-fiction was once deemed an endangered species on television, yet there is a seeming onslaught of genre programming--all set aboard space stations.

Some have claimed plagarism as DEEP SPACE NINE, BABYLON 5 and SPACE RANGERS battle for the hearts, minds and Nielson ratings of viewers. However, it should come as no surprise that producers have become drawn to these stationary venues for their science-fiction series.

With the increasing demand for feature-quality production values and action, and with budgets now hovering near $2 million an episode, sending large casts off in search of adventure in the final frontier had become a prohibitively expensive affair. By setting their respective shows onboard space stations, brave new worlds can be eschewed for the standing sets, thus allowing for inner exploration of less expensive character relationships as opposed to the outward seeking voyages of a starship which charts brand new soundstages every week.

The science-fiction worlds of DEEP SPACE, BABYLON 5 and SPACE RANGERS are a natural reflection of our own contemporary science which, rather than set its sights on the moon or Mars, has instead chosen to construct the first American manned space station since Skylab, the Freedom, which is still imperiled by possible Congressional budget cuts to NASA.

Behind all three shows are strong and creative talents bringing their own unique science-fiction visions to the screen. DEEP SPACE is captained by the talented keeper's of the STAR TREK flame, Rick Berman and Michael Piller, who have managed to make NEXT GENERATION the sensation of first run syndication and the model against which all future science-fiction television programming will be judged.

With DEEP SPACE they can finally imprint their distinctive talents onto the STAR TREK universe, boldly exploring nooks and crannies of a 24th century Gene Roddenberry never dreamed existed. J. Michael Straczynski, a longtime science-fiction fan and veteran of shows like CAPTAIN POWER and THE NEW TWILIGHT ZONE, is realizing a long held dream in bringing BABYLON 5, a gritty and dark story of the warring five Federations being brought together by the hope of a better tomorrow, to the screen. And, last but not least, the creative talents behind ROBIN HOOD: PRINCE OF THIEVES and BACKDRAFT are bringing the genre back to network television with SPACE RANGERS, which eschews high-technology for dramatic space opera.

Some have compared the various series, wondering which one's the best and which will endure. In fact, there's no reason not to hope that they will *all* succeed. In a television universe where science-fiction has been a casualty of the desire of advertisers to reach the broadest audience possible, while networks try to trim costs by relying on less expensive reality-based and sitcom fare, the presence of three ambitious science-fiction vehicles is a treat for fans of the genre. Instead of pitting these three programs against each other like competitors in gladiatorial games, they should embrace all three series hoping for a new science-fiction renaissance on television.

With former Paramount Studios and NBC chief Brandon Tartikoff's comments that if he were running a network today he would program science-fiction fare, the possibility of the glory days of the science-fiction genre on television may be upon us again.

In EXPLORING DEEP SPACE AND BEYOND we'll examine all three of these ambitious new shows along with the history of space stations in science and science-fiction written by noted author Mitchell Rubinstein. Additionally, we'll look at the complex machinations that result in what you see on the screen.

Together, the writers, cast and crew discuss their hopes, dreams and aspirations for the future of both their respective series and man's continuing drive to colonize the cosmos.

MARK A. ALTMAN
April 1993

PROLOGUE

Science fiction and science fact have always run a somewhat parallel course, enjoying many fortuitous collisions along the way. What may have previously been the stuff of fantasy can quickly become hard fact and with the astounding rate of technological advance, elements of modern science are often key parts of today's science fiction. The nearly maniacal fixation of the cyberpunk "movement" on biotechnology is a good example of this.

Some of SF's greatest moments involve these, often occurring occasions of convergence between fact and fantasy. One of the best (though nobody seems to know for sure whether or not it is true) involved one of science fiction's best known editors and authors, John Campbell, who in the mid 1940's was publishing many stories involving the possible military uses of Uranium 235.

SF writers knew of Fermi's early fission experiments and extrapolated the possibility of releasing almost unlimited amounts of explosive energy. Atom bomb stories were the rage in the pulp magazines while the Manhattan Project was still top secret. As far as they knew, the writers were exploring totally fictional territory. The public at large was unaware of the work going on in New Mexico, and the government preferred that it stay that way. The story goes that the F.B.I. paid Campbell a visit to ask him to please stop publishing the stories. He pointed out to them that putting an abrupt halt to the stories would be more likely to give away the truth than would allowing them to continue, and the government relented. The F.B.I. has always denied the story.

Space stations and their role in the manned exploration of our solar system have been central points in many of science fiction's greatest works, both literary and cinematic. Clarke, Asimov, Heinlein, Bradbury, Niven and countless others have used them in various incarnations either as peripheral props or as central characters in literally thousands of short stories and novels. There were many reasons for this.

First is that space stations have played a relatively minor role in the actual exploration of our solar system. So the risk of having your story contradicted by the actuality is quite low. Also, the basic technology, with a few notable exceptions we will get to later, is really very simple. Any writer with a few engineering tables and a pocket calculator (or back in the 1940's a slide rule) could calculate dimensions and orbits for just about any type of space contraption he or she could dream up.

The barriers to the actual use of space stations were always economic and political. Technology which exists but is not practical is always fertile ground for fictional exploration. All one need do is dream up a plot or environment in which it would be practical, and start clacking away at the typewriter. The harsh and often dull realities of Skylab, Soyuz and Mir would pale in comparison.

Skylab was launched in May, 1973 as the first attempt by the United States to establish a base for the purpose of testing Man's ability to live and work in space. It lasted about six years and served mostly to demonstrate just how many things can go wrong on a single project, and that in the unforgiving environment of space there is much less to be taken for granted.

In September of 1973, on a mission involving Alan Bean, Jack Lousma and Owen Garriot, half of the command module's thrusters failed. The exercise nearly had to be scrapped and a rescue mission mounted.

Garriot did establish himself as the world's first orbiting practical joker. He played taped messages from his wife over the radio to mission control, all but convincing them that the astronauts had a woman on the station with them.

Later that winter the station's star tracker failed completely and had to be shut down. The experiments lagged behind and a special EVA had to be mounted to repair a damaged antenna. Skylab did succeed in photographing solar flares from space for the first time and also in gathering a great deal of meteorological data. Additionally, they proved that spiders could spin webs in zero gravity.

Miscalculations and mounting technical failures caused Skylab's orbit to deteriorate. It re-entered the Earth's atmosphere and burned up over the Indian Ocean on July 11th, 1979.

The Soviets' accomplishments in space station research have always been thought to be of greater dimension than those of the United States, due in part to a differing set of priorities. N.A.S.A had won the race to the moon and it was partly out of a desire to even the score that the C.C.C.P. devoted such vast resources to the Soyuz and Mir projects. Soviet secrecy has always kept many of the more interesting details of the missions from public view, though they unquestionably hold the endurance record for keeping humans in space.

Fictional space stations have usually enjoyed more trouble free operation than their real life counterparts, except of course when trouble fits nicely into the plot. Some of the first hard fiction involving space stations in a central role was offered by a writer named George O. Smith, in a series of short stories published in "Astounding" in the late 1940's. The stories involved the Venus Equilateral relay station, a mile long orbiting communications platform whose purpose was to relay interplanetary messages around the sun. The station was manned by a collection of oddball geniuses who were constantly being called upon to solve all the problems in the solar system.

This might not seem like the most original setup. What made the stories different was Smith's effort to be realistic and technologically accurate. In 1945 Arthur C. Clarke had first proposed the idea of communications satellites and like Smith, he envisioned huge manned platforms which would serve many functions, not the miniature automatons such as Telstar and its descendants.

With this in mind, Smith, who had an engineering degree, a great sense of humor and a flare for the dramatic, wrote stories about life in space which were unsurpassed in technical accuracy--1940's technical accuracy that is. Reading them today one is reminded of a cruel truth in science fiction writing; the more detailed and accurate your science is, the more rapidly you are overtaken by the relentless march of technological advance.

Venus Equilateral flew in the days before computers existed in any practical sense, before printed circuits, before touch-tone phones, jet aircraft and years before the transistor was even invented. Smith's was a world of vacuum tubes and crystal radio sets. His inventions, most of which would be considered fantastic even today, were all based on science which now seems almost childish.

Yet when terrorists threatened to attack the station, electron guns were fashioned out of giant vacuum tubes. No lasers. When they needed to build a matter transporter (a concept which long preceded STAR TREK), it was constructed from cathodes, anodes, coiled power transformers and lots of copper wire. Radio signals were received and amplified without the aid of computer enhancement and were not recorded, as audio tape didn't even exist. Meticulous as he tried to be, Smith's stories were outdated by 1950. Asimov was another writer who loathed inaccurate science and agonized over this same problem. In later editions of some of his earlier works he included a disclaimer in the introduction, explaining that the march of time could even catch up with him, and that we should try to enjoy the stories anyway.

But the Venus Equilateral stories were the first to address many of the standard difficulties associated with space station life. The ship had the approximate proportions of a coffee can and had to be spun on its axis for gravity, resulting in a pseudo-gravity which lessened progressively as one neared the axis of rotation. There were no "gravity generators" or other such nonsense. Life support systems, an oldie but a goodie when it comes to conjuring up a good space disaster, were centered around a giant garden of foliage specifically designed to absorb carbon dioxide and produce oxygen.

In one story a visiting bureaucrat, not understanding the garden's significance, has all of the greenery thrown out the hatch. If you want to know how they solved *that* little problem, the stories exist (eleven of them if I remember correctly) in an anthology called THE COMPLETE VENUS EQUILATERAL. The book's first edition was introduced by Arthur C. Clarke himself, and it is one of the few cases in which a book has an introduction written by someone you've actually heard of.

Smith's technical material may be outdated, but his characters felt the loneliness and isolation of space station life, the feeling of being men and women without a country (or planet), of being citizens of space, and the closeness of having to depend for their very lives on the people around them. These are all things which have been described repeatedly and in detail by real astronauts and cosmonauts even today, almost fifty years after Smith's stories were set to paper.

Remember that good science fiction must be, above all, good fiction. I still re-read the Venus Equilateral stories occasionally and it is not for the flawed science but rather for Smith's excellent characterizations and his ability to tell great stories. Without this, his work would be no more than outdated technical treatise, as a great deal of modern science fiction eventually becomes.

But space stations need not be of human origin. Several SF classics center on the exploration of alien constructions, which actually presents a different set of challenges to the writer. Anything which seems like it could not exist in our world can be attributed to advanced alien technology, far in advance of our own. In this subgenre imaginations run wild, dreaming up some of science fiction's most spectacular creations.

One such monstrosity was the Ringworld, about which Larry Niven wrote a novel in 1970 and which he expanded upon ten years later in THE RINGWORLD ENGINEERS.. Ringworld was a space station only in the loosest sense of the word. A multimillion mile long ribbon constructed circumfirentially around a sun and revolving for gravity, it is a habitat containing roughly three million times the surface area of the Earth, and the mass of the planet Jupiter. People could live on the inner surface, with the sun always at high noon and thousand mile high walls to keep the air from spilling out into space.

Niven and many others maintain that such a structure is theoretically possible to construct, and the books were indeed masterpieces of technological fantasy. They have always been popular with fans of hard SF (that is, science fiction in which the author maintains at least a passing effort at being accurate about his/her science.) Niven was sent hundreds of letters by eager fans, many of them scientists and engineers, outlining problems and defects in Ringworld's design. At one science fiction convention a group of M.I.T. students set up a chant of "The Ringworld is unstable!" Niven corrected many of the problems in the book's second addition and expanded upon them in THE RINGWORLD ENGINEERS.

Clarke's RENDEZVOUS WITH RAMA (1973) is the other classic SF novel involving an Alien space station and is in many ways the most mysterious. Clarke usually wrote stories which shared an upsetting similarity with real life, namely that the all the puzzles do not get solved. The end of a Clarke story always leaves you with a nagging feeling that you've missed something and you want to know more.

RENDEZVOUS WITH RAMA centers on a giant alien ship discovered hurtling towards us from the far reaches of space. The featureless craft, shaped like an immense water heater, is about forty miles long, and its course will soon see it flying out of the solar system forever. An exploratory mission is hurriedly mounted. Once inside, the crew of the research ship Endeavor have surprises in store for them unlike anything written about before or since.

Inside Rama (the name comes from Hindu mythology) the wonders of a craft spun on its axis for gravity are completely explored. The cylindrical hull is both the floor under their feet and the sky over their heads. A cylindrical glacier separates one end of the frozen ship from the other. But Clarke does not spring all his wonders on us at once. When the crew enters Rama it is completely dark. They soon realize that the apparently functionless trenches running the length of the ship are actually linear suns, and Rama is flooded with light. Then, as it nears the sun, the deep freeze encasing the ship begins to thaw. The cylindrical glacier melts into a cylindrical sea with waves that run circumfirentially without end. Life comes to Rama as well in the form of three armed biological robots (biots). But again, Clarke's human drama mixes with the wonderment, in some of his best storytelling since his novelization of 2001.

At one point, the only way to pass the cylindrical sea to Rama's distant tip is for one of the explorers to take a human powered aircraft up to the region of zero gravity and fly straight down the ship's axis. His journey is a modernized Odyssey in and of itself and were the book not spectacular from start to finish would be worth reading for this passage alone. I would give away little else in case you have not read it and are planning to do so.

These are, again, just a few terribly isolated examples of the uses of space stations in literature. There are countless others in which they are used as a setting or plot device without being central to the story.

Probably the ultimate space station concept is the enclosed universe story, which has been written by many authors. The best known version is Heinlein's story "Universe" (1939), which he later expanded into the novel ORPHANS OF THE SKY (1963). Heinlein did not originate the concept as many science fiction fans believe, though he can be credited with popularizing it enormously. It had been done years before by Don Wilcox, and the premise has been borrowed by, among others, Alex Panchent and Harry Harrison.

The concept is that of the giant ark, space station, colony ship, whatever, which is bound for the stars but suffers some disastrous mishap. The ship is thrown off course and wanders aimlessly through space. Years later the passengers' descendants are alive and well but they have forgotten Earth, forgotten their mission and have in fact forgotten that they are on a space ship. To them the universe is but a few miles long and made out of metal. Religions are born to explain how the ship came into being and what its purpose might be.

In Heinlein's version a young adventurer exploring the forgotten upper decks happens upon a room from which the stars can be seen and he slowly learns the truth of his situation. As always, Heinlein puts things in a historical context. He parallels his hero's plight with that of Galileo facing his Catholic inquisitors and trying to convince them that the universe is not as Ptolemy stated, with the Earth motionless at the center and all else revolving around it. In UNIVERSE, he must convince the ship's elders that the ship is actually moving and that outside its walls is a space vast beyond all comprehension. The elders of course brand him a heretic and force him into submission. In one of his most melodramatic moments Heinlein has his beaten protagonist mutter "nevertheless, it still moves", virtually a direct quote from Galileo at his own inquisition.

Another version of the enclosed universe story had not nearly so successful a course. In the early 1970's, Harlan Ellison sold a concept to 20th Century Fox to do a television series in a setting similar to that of UNIVERSE. The characters' adventures and their steps toward discovering the nature of their predicament constituted the plot. The eventual goal was to have them discover the control room and realize they are on an interstellar runaway train. Ellison once described the concept as doing THE FUGITIVE in space.

Now Ellison is widely regarded as the John Mcenroe of science fiction. That is, he is talented almost beyond what seems humanly possible and is at the same time a nearly unendurable pain in the ass. Sadly, a few simple facts conspired against him and turned a decent idea into some of the most inane, embarrassing crap ever shown on television.

Fact one: Television producers and writers are rarely science fiction fans and have little or no concept of what makes science fiction work or not work. Second: said producers and writers are usually virtually illiterate when it comes to technical matters, rendering them capable of errors which would make FLASH GORDON look like a documentary. Lastly: Television producers are concerned primarily with playing it safe, and SF is all about taking chances.

What Ellison found was that his ideas were being diluted, slowly at first, and he did not have control over who was doing the writing. This turned out to be a major disaster. The lowest of politics played into the casting of the show, resulting in the lead being played by Keir ("Open the pod bay doors, Hal") Dullea, one of the most stone faced and least charismatic actors imaginable. Ellison had envisioned someone like Robert Blake or Walter Koenig as his leading man. Eventually disappointment piled on disappointment to the point where Ellison was unwilling even to have his name associated with the project.

It is unlikely that you will ever see the show, called THE STARLOST. I'm told it is running in syndication in a few cities when there is room at 2:30 A.M. between infomercials. If you do see it you will also see the name Cordwainer Bird in the credits. That is Ellison's pseudonym and when asked why he chose that particular name he said it was his way of symbolically giving "the bird" to the purveyors of mediocrity who had destroyed his show.

Those who attempt to put SF on film have reasons for utilizing space stations that novelists rarely need to worry about. It is a way of limiting the environment and bringing the scope of the project down to a manageable level. You do not need to worry about creating a whole new planet and concomitant culture, ecology, history etc.

In the case of a T.V. series it allows you to build only a few standing sets which can then be used over and over again, thus saving money. This is naturally the case in the less imaginative, more formula shows such as SPACE 1999, THE STARLOST, BUCK ROGERS and the like.

Of course, even spending $35 million on a film does not render you immune from shear idiocy, as the creators of the James Bond film MOONRAKER must surely know. Their orbiting space station, belonging to yet another billionaire megalomaniac, is about the most ludicrous in recent memory. It rotates to produce gravity but when the rotation is halted the characters are still able to walk around. When it does rotate, the zero gravity area is the furthest from the axis of rotation, quite the opposite of reality. It was assembled in space undetected by Earth based radar, which is capable of tracking anything in orbit larger than a basketball.

To be fair of course, it's only a Bond film. They've never been exactly famous for their realism.

In the films written and produced by the true craftsmen of science fiction filmmaking and in whose hands the genre attains its highest level, space stations have been used realistically and creatively. In 2001, Stanley Kubrick used them as a metaphor for Man's never ending effort to throw something higher than anyone has before. If that sounds like pretentious B.S., rent the film and examine closely the point where the scene shifts from prehistory to the future.

With any luck the coming generations of science fiction writers and fans will continue to use space stations in new and interesting ways, and remember that the kinds of characters which will live in them are far more important than the frail orbiting shells they occupy.

And when, as inevitably occurs, reality catches up once again, we will indeed have a world with such things in it as no visionaries, other than science fiction writers, had ever forseen.

Mitchell Rubinstein
January, 1993

CHAPTER ONE
Adventures in Deep Space

With the success of STAR TREK it seemed inevitable that Paramount would consider the idea of a spin-off. After all, the last chapter of the feature film franchise had been written and NEXT GENERATION was winding its way into its latter seasons with impending contract negotiations jeopardizing the future of the show. Ironically, however, it wasn't what made NEXT GENERATION a success that was the creative impetus for the new series, but what *didn't*. In creating the STAR TREK sister series, Co-Creators Rick Berman and Michael Piller realized that they would need to address the liabilities of a universe in which interpersonal conflict was anathema. As a result, DEEP SPACE NINE is a world populated by aliens from across the galaxy, only some of them being Starfleet officers. The world they inhabit is gritty and alien, unlike the sterile and nearly-perfect utopia within the confines of a starship.

"It's an alien space station that doesn't work the way they want it to, so we've created a lot of conflict," insists Rick Berman about the newly assembled ensemble of DEEP SPACE NINE. "At the same time our core characters are Starfleet officers; Sisko, O'Brien, the doctor and Dax in no way vary from THE NEXT GENERATION in terms of the lack of conflict among themselves. That was a rule that we had to follow. We needed to create a series that wasn't a franchise based on a people aboard a starship because we knew there would be a couple of years of overlap between the two series."

Some fans have expressed concern over the fact that after the death of Gene Roddenberry, the man with the vision who created the show, STAR TREK's magic could not be recaptured. However, as Herman Zimmerman, DEEP SPACE's production designer and a veteran of the start-up of NEXT GENERATION points out, the STAR TREK universe has been interpeted by many creative individuals who have inherited the concepts created by Roddenberry over its 25 year plus existence.

"From my point of view Gene Roddenberry created, without being maudlin, an eternal idealization of the future," says Zimmerman, who designed the original sets for NEXT GENERATION as well as THE FINAL FRONTIER and THE UNDISCOVERED COUNTRY feature films. "The characters that he created came out of his imagination pretty much whole cloth. You could compare 'The Cage' to 'The Sign of Four' that was written by Arthur Conan Doyle. Sherlock Holmes and Watson and Moriarity and La Strade and the Baker Street Irregulars have a charm and an identity that is immediately discernible from that very first novel. Seventy years later a fellow named Nick Meyer can take the same characters and write a very believable Arthur Conan Doyle story, maybe even better, but using all those same characters and ideas and call it THE SEVEN PERCENT SOLUTION.

"Gene Roddenberry created Kirk and Spock and McCoy, Uhura, Sulu, Chekov, Picard, Riker, Troi, etc. and when they were first introduced to the audience, just like those characters from Arthur Conan Doyle, they were whole. They haven't changed, [though] they may have grown. They've been interpreted and that's the beauty of Gene's vision from his positive view of the future and his ability to mix and match personalities that play well together. I think any good director, writer, producer can take those criteria, those characters, that idea, that vision and make it work. Within that we have the grittiness that Nicholas Meyer prefers, the Hyatt Regency approach that Gene liked in the NEXT GENERATION and we have the bizarre, darker alien version of the stories in DEEP SPACE NINE. Mike Okuda and I philosophize once in a while and he said something very poignant when we were probably halfway through the set construction of the first two hour, and very heavily into doing all the details. He said it's beginning to have a life of it's own. STAR TREK from the very beginning has had that snowball effect. It has evolved and it does have a life of its own and we'll see it for many more years in the future."

In fact, the STAR TREK purists who would use the so-called "darker" TREK of DEEP SPACE NINE to decry the new series as blasepheming Gene Roddenberry's 26-year-old vision would be wrong. DEEP SPACE NINE is more faithful to the original STAR TREK premise than even THE NEXT GENERATION has been. DEEP SPACE NINE revives the interpersonal conflict and witty banter of the classic show's popular triumverate of Kirk, Spock and McCoy, while retaining the elements of the new show that have made it one of the most successful series on television.

Although as anyone familar with the production of STAR TREK: THE NEXT GENERATION would readily attest it's Rick Berman who has been the real great bird behind its phenemonal success, aided and abetted by his Co-Executive Producer Michael Piller who has overseen the writing staff of the show since its third year. But Berman is the one who successfully moved the series through early production trmoil, and for the last several years turned it into a critical and ratings success. He is the man that Paramount has entrusted their leading tent pole and studio franchise; he is the heir to the Roddenberry universe.

Whether you like NEXT GENERATION or not, the show has borne the distinctive imprint of Berman whose meticulous attention to detail has kept him immersed in the day to day running of the show since his elevation second season to Executive Producer, following Bob Justman's retirement. But now, with DEEP SPACE NINE, Berman has been put in the uncomfortable position of relinquishing his tight control over NEXT GENERATION in order to oversee the launch of its sister series.

"When I was in charge of one of these television shows it was taking up all of my time," says Berman. "I was working 50-60 hours a week. Now I've got two shows and I can't work 100-120 hours a week. What I have had to do is start delegating things that I normally have not been willing to delegate--and it's a bitch. The attention that I put into the scripts and the rewrites and the polishing of the scripts on NEXT GENERATION is something that is very difficult for me to walk away from. The work that I do in the cutting room is difficult as well, but I'm finding that I can walk away from it to a small degree. On NEXT GENERATION, up until last season, I would normally put 15 hours of cutting time into a picture until it was locked. Now I'm probably putting 5 hours as opposed to 15 and I'm putting a lot less time into the rewriting of the NEXT GENERATION episodes. I've found ways of working with [NEXT GENERATION Co-Executive Producer] Jeri Taylor that I think are comfortable and save some time."

Fortunately for Berman, the staff he has put together over the last several years has functioned extremely efficiently, thus allowing him to delegate responsibilities that were once exclusively his domain. This he labels as one of his greatest accomplishments on the show. Berman, unlike Roddenberry, has managed to ride herd over those involved with the creation of the STAR TREK universe without alienating the myriad individuals that Roddenberry did.

"I've got over 300 people working for me and I don't think there's a television show in L.A. right now that has the less attrition than we have," says Berman. "We have the same teams of people working on the show that we did five years ago with very few exceptions. On STAR TREK: THE NEXT GENERATION we have seven actors. Usually after six years of a series, the actors are all at each others' throats, they are at the directors' throats and the producers' throats. It's ugly. Our actors and myself have as warm and healthy a creative rapport as we had in the beginning. The same is true of the myriad people involved with the production of the show. Maintaining that delicate balance of keeping the place running responsibly, keeping people happy and feeling like they're part of the creative process, and smiling is my biggest challenge and I think it's worked out very well."

Berman's complete autonomy over the STAR TREK universe has been ceded on DEEP SPACE NINE where he rules, albeit benevolently, in tandem with Michael Piller, the series' co-creator.

"We don't do anything without Berman and Piller's approval," says production designer Herman Zimmerman. "They know where this series is going and we make all sorts of elaborate proposals based on what we think from our imagination the scripts require. But in the final analysis it is their guiding hand that says yes or no to any given idea."

"I am a writer," says Piller. "I live in a world of imagination, just ask my wife. I depend enormously on Rick's intuitions and his talents in production, and I know Rick depends a great deal on Herman's [Zimmerman]. In all of the productions and the editing and the look of the show, I am there as another voice, thinking, offering my best wisdom and counsel, but I depend a great deal on Mr. Berman for those things.

Piller and Berman's deliberations, which have already had an effect on determining the look of the show as well as the casting due to their different tastes, lie in stark contrast to their relationship on NEXT GENERATION, where Berman always has the final word. This was evidenced by their well-documented disagreement over the ending of the fifth season episode "Perfect Mate" on NEXT GENERATION, in which Berman overruled Piller's proposed ending for the episode in which Picard disrupts the wedding ceremony between the beautiful mesamorph and Par Lenor.

"The bottom line is that I work *for* Rick on THE NEXT GENERATION and I work *with* Rick on DEEP SPACE NINE," says Piller. "Our working relationship is virtually identical except that when a decision of critical importance has to be made we really reach a consensus. On DEEP SPACE NINE sometimes I win and sometimes he wins....he *always* wins on THE NEXT GENERATION."

In contrasting their two personalities, Berman points out that Piller is far more introspective and self-critical. This is reflected in Piller's harsh assessment of TREK's fifth season as well as early drafts of the DEEP SPACE NINE opener. "Michael's tougher on himself than I am," offers Berman. "We rarely disagree on script points. We spend a lot of time with writers making scripts work after first drafts come in, and he and I rarely disagree. I rarely disagree with him in terms of casting and in terms of production."

In examining the first few months of DEEP SPACE NINE's production, Piller is pleased with the course the show has taken.

"It's been a blessed project," he says. "I hope blessings continue. We wrote a story, the studio loved it. I wrote a script and everybody seemed to love it. We cast a group of actors that are delightful. Colm Meaney told Rick [Berman] that he hasn't worked with a group of actors this fine since he was in the Abbey. I was able to hire Ira Behr who was my key man in to be able to execute this plan. Peter came over from NEXT GENERATION as the one tool that I was willing to rob the NEXT GENERATION of, and leave the THE NEXT GENERATION with the guidance of Jeri Taylor. She's done a marvelous job and that's worked out. When it comes down to it, everyone seems to be able to execute and Rick and I support each other marvelously. We care a great deal about what we're doing and the studio couldn't be more supportive. I'm the guy who's always sort of looking over his shoulder for the footsteps and I haven't heard them yet."

Although DEEP SPACE NINE is a non-moving station seemingly offering a finite number of story possibilities, Piller suggests that it's easier to come up with plotlines for DEEP SPACE than it has been for NEXT GENERATION.

"We can still get into a Runabout and go anywhere we want," says Piller of the ship's mini-starships which take the crew through the wormhole into the Gamma quadrant. "What we have here that we don't have on the Enterprise is a community that's beyond a life business. We have people at play on the Promenade and at Quark's, and people who are not involved directly in the running of the Starfleet operation who are main characters on the show. That makes it easier."

Others disagree, one source close to the production suggesting, "It's only a matter of time before they strap warp engines onto that baby and let her fly because it's impossible to keep coming up with stories set aboard a space station."

The dilemma, admits Piller, is avoiding the fact that 200 stories that have been told in TREK's previous incarnations in both the 60's and on the NEXT GENERATION. "The bottom line is that the kind of stories that work on the NEXT GENERATION are the same kind that we want to tell on DEEP SPACE NINE," says Piller. "But we'll tell those stories illuminating different characters and different alien groups, but still explore the human condition and use the metaphors that work so well. It's the universe of science-fiction and the universe of Gene Roddenberry. We cannot do stories on DEEP SPACE NINE that wouldn't work on the other two STAR TREK shows. The problems are the same. We can't repeat ourselves. We have to come up with fresh and original material and it's very, very difficult."

CHAPTER TWO
Creating Deep Space

After working together successfully for a number of years, Rick Berman and Michael Piller had became intrigued with the idea of creating and producing their own show, which would not necessarily take place in the STAR TREK universe.

"Michael had been working with me for two years and he and I had lunch together very often. We started talking about developing other television series," recalls Berman. "We talked about STAR TREK spin-offs and we talked about a lot of other shows as well. There were many, many series we discussed. The only one that was really a spin-off was DEEP SPACE NINE. I went to Gene and mentioned we were thinking about a spin-off and he said great and that we should talk about it sometime. Unfortunately, we never did because he was not well then and he got worse and worse."

Ironically, former Paramount studio chief Brandon Tartikoff summoned Berman to his office shortly thereafter to discuss creating a new show for the studio.

"I got a call from Brandon who brought me into his office with John Pike and said, 'I would like you to create another television show for us,'" says Berman. "He said he wanted a science-fiction show and I said 'You mean a STAR TREK show?' and he said, 'No, I don't care if it's STAR TREK. I want another science-fiction show I can say is being created by the guy who's been bringing you STAR TREK: THE NEXT GENERATION for the last five years.' I told Brandon that I had been working with Mike Piller on a number of ideas. It was one of those 'Oh, and by the way, I just happen to have one right here.' So Mike and I started talking again. At that point there was no question that the person I wanted to bring in to work on something like this was Michael and it basically came down to two of the ideas we had been playing with."

Michael Piller explains that the studio was initially against doing another STAR TREK series, but was eventually won over by the premise for the proposed spin-off. Among the ideas Piller and Berman had toyed with were the original premise for DEEP SPACE NINE, involving a space station on the outer fringes of Federation space, and one which was a science-fiction series set during medieval times on earth.

"We decided on DEEP SPACE NINE, in a very fledgling stage, and we went to the studio guys and laid out a pretty general idea. They said go and work on it and we spent a number of months coming up with the premise before the story was written with the earliest bible of the show; what the location would be, what the backstory would be and the studio said go for it."

With the studio greenlighting production, Piller and Berman spent a lot of late nights together devising the final premise for the series which, unlike the prior two STAR

TREK series, would *not* take place on a Federation starship. "Mike and I knew that if we were ever going to do another STAR TREK show it would have to take place somewhere where adventure could come to us as opposed to us going to adventure. That's why we came up with the idea of a wormhole."

Berman is adamant that the reason for setting the series on a space station was not a cost-related decision. Yet conventional logic would suggest that a stationary locale would be a money saver over the adventures of a starship whose mandate was to explore brave new worlds.

"It had nothing to do with budget," says Berman. "DEEP SPACE is going to be more expensive than any show Paramount's ever done. You can't have two shows on the air with people on starships. We needed to come up with something new and put 24th century people into a new environment. If you can't be in a vehicle that's taking you to where adventure is then you have to put yourself somewhere where adventure comes to you. The idea of the wormhole titillated us and then adding to that the whole Bajoran backstory, which Michael and I had created a year ago."

The establishment of the Bajoran culture was done in the early fifth season episode, "Ensign Ro" in which Piller and Berman introduced the character of Ro Laren, played by Michelle Forbes. Ro is a disgraced Starfleet officer and member of a race that has been forced from their home planet by the Cardassians, the newest malevolent TREK baddies (first seen in fourth season's "The Wounded") with whom the Federation has an uneasy truce.

"We must have had 50 meetings before we felt comfortable with what we had come up with," says Berman. "It's grown the way a child grows from something that is young and simple to something that is more complex. The premise has never made a major left or right turn. The characters and backstory have become more focused, the settings, the people and the interrelationships. I'm sure a year from now it will be much richer than it is today."

Ultimately, the most important aspect of the new series for the producers was making the new show less constraining in terms of allowing interpersonal conflict between the characters.

"The problem with STAR TREK: THE NEXT GENERATION is Gene created a group of characters that he purposely chose not to allow conflict between," says Berman. "Starfleet officers cannot be in conflict, thus it's murderous to write these shows because there is no good drama without conflict and the conflict has to come from outside the group."

In order to bring conflict to the 24th century without violating the Roddenberry dictum governing his universe, Berman and Piller agreed to introduce non-Starfleet personnel into the mix who aren't governed by the same set of constraints that Federation officers had been in the previous series.

"What we wanted to do was set out to do something that was somewhat paradoxical--bring conflict but not break away from Gene's rules," says Berman. "They still play paramount importance in what we're doing. We created an environment where Starfleet officers were in a location that they weren't happy about being in, and they were in a location where the people who lived there weren't all that happy about them being there. We also created a situation where we had people who were members of our core group who were not Starfleet: the security shape shifter Odo, the Bajoran major Kira, the bartender Quark. A group of our integral people are not Starfleet officers, and the ones that are Starfleet officers aren't crazy about where they are so we have a lot of frustration and conflict."

Michael Piller disagrees that the emphasis on Bajoran spirituality and secular beliefs goes against the atheist, anti-religious beliefs of Roddenberry.

"I don't think it goes against Gene," he says. "If he was still with us--and he's still on our shoulders as we think about these conceptual issues--I don't think it would bother him one bit. What he felt very strongly about is that humans, and to some degree Federation members, had a humanist attitude; logic and reality. His humans do not overtly celebrate religious beliefs. What we have simply done in creating an environment that will bring conflict to our people, which we wanted to desperately do, was to put a group of people with a group of aliens that are different than we are; who had a difference and a conflict with our humanist beliefs. By giving them strong spiritual mystical orbs and prophet worship, it forces our humanist people to deal with another alien race that is as different from us as the Klingons are. They're different in the spiritually of their existence. We're saying if there's a problem here, let's fix the problem and they're saying the prophets have to be satisfied and that causes conflict.

"Gene would be the first to tell you it doesn't matter what alien race you're talking about, how hideous they seem to be, there are no bad aliens. Each of them have a culture within itself which must be defined, recognized and appreciated for what it is. We're simply creating a new alien race with a new set of circumstances and not changing Gene's vision of what humanity is in the 24th century. We're simply showing how we are affected by that conflict with that alien race."

"I think Piller and Rick are both in a very good place," says DEEP SPACE writer/producer Ira Steven Behr, a veteran of STAR TREK: THE NEXT GENERATION who was lured back into the fold with the prospect of working on a harder-edged TREK. "With all the hassles of doing two shows and mistakes and all the things that happen, we still get along and it's been fun. I kept saying to Mike and Rick I don't want to go back and do STAR TREK again. Good or bad, they kept saying, 'This is going to be a different show, we're really trying to keep it in the whole STAR TREK ethos but we're going to make this a different show.' And I'm thinking this is easy to say, but once you've done something it's tough to suddenly shift gears and do this other thing and do them both at the same time. I was a bit skeptical , but then I read the pilot, and I started to say 'Hmm, this has some potential.'

"What I was figuring was if you're going to have two hours of STAR TREK on a week, not counting all those repeats, they really have to be different than each other. People are getting their orgasm off watching THE NEXT GENERATION, once a week is enough for most people. We're asking them to come again and in order to do that you have to give them different stuff. I think that's what we're doing and as I sit there and watch dailies, I keep saying to Rick and Michael, people are going to be surprised by this show."

Behr echoes the party line that the show isn't darker, simply different....perhaps reflected in its grittier *mis en scene* and tone.

"This isn't an angst ridden, existential show," adds Behr. "I'm not trying to make it more than it is. It's still an hour of television, it's still an hour of STAR TREK television. But there's definite conflict and there are characters who are carrying all kinds of things around with them and I'm not just talking about Sisko losing his wife, which is a nice television convention. There's people like Odo and Kira who are intensely driven people with things they have to deal with. You end up watching a lot of scenes where people are not agreeing with each other and the look of the show has a feeling that's a lot different in the lighting and the architecture than THE NEXT GENERATION."

Like THE NEXT GENERATION, DEEP SPACE NINE shoots on three soundstages on the Paramount lot, occasionally venturing off the studio grounds for location shooting. The stations' operation's center, which boasts a science station, the Cardassian equivalent of the captain's ready room, a replicator, transporter pad and environmental controls, is located on Stage 4 along with crew quarters, station corridor's and the station's docking bay and launch pads. Adjacent to Stage 4 is the home of the Promenade, which houses the sexual holosuites and Quark's bar.

"It's a space station that's in a way smaller than the Enterprise," says Herman Zimmerman. "It occupies a larger volume of space but the actual structure is mostly space and not interior volume. It has the sense of being more enclosed except for the Promenade, which is a larger stage. It's more like the interior of a submarine, a nice atomic submarine mind you, but a submarine nonetheless."

For Berman, Zimmerman was a natural choice for designing the new show's alien look. His close collaboration with the production designer and Piller has helped firmly entrench DEEP SPACE NINE as the cutting edge of televised science-fiction, while also allowing Zimmerman creative freedom.

"Herman and I have been close for many years, even after he left the show," says Berman. "I knew I wanted to bring Herman into this from the start, and the exterior of the station was something that we spent a lot of time on. There were dozens of designs, most of which I didn't like. Some of which Michael liked and I didn't, others I liked and Michael did. Finally, we came up with an idea that worked very nicely and constantly changed that. As far as the interior designs, we knew we wanted the Promenade and a big area that had all the shops and stores and a bar, and let Herman go about his magical way."

Once coming onboard, Zimmerman immediately began working on concepts for the fledgling series--despite the fact that initially he had very little to work from since Berman and Piller were still refining their concepts as to what the show would be.

"The first thing I had to do was find out what the scripts were going to be like and there was some hesitation about that," says Zimmerman. "I spent quite a few weeks working without any script, just story ideas and what we thought the exterior of the station would look like. The producers were so heavily involved with the tail-end of the fifth season on NEXT GENERATION that I was pretty much left to my own devices. I probably have seven inches of single spaced paper stacked with drawings that never came about. Ideas that came and went as we got closer to an agreement on what the show should be about and what the station should look like and what sort of people we were going to put into this environment. Some of the ideas from the early days were useful and quite a few of them were not. It was an interesting and creative time for me."

Unlike his early work on the NEXT GENERATION in which Zimmerman updated the established sets of the original series and the feature films, DEEP SPACE NINE was a blank slate that forced the designer to envision totally new TREK concepts.

"First we worked on what the exterior of the station would look like up until March of this year. Then we were very heavily into designing what the exterior would look like and we went through a number of ramifications. At first, Berman and Piller thought the station should be falling apart and in a very bad state of disrepair showing the effects of time and neglect and so on. But as we started developing sketches for what that kind of a station would look like, none of us liked it. We were saying to ourselves this is space, the final frontier, 400 years in the future and we should be as high tech and slick and believable in scientific terms as possible. We did a fairly sharp 180 and went to another concept."

It was decided that since the station was built by Bajoran slave labor for use by the Cardassians in strip mining the planet Bajor of its precious mineral resources, a Cardassian influence would be incorporated into the design of the station.

"The Cardassians as a race have been seen in NEXT GENERATION in a couple of episodes. Where they've been seen their make-up and their costume had already been developed. Bob Blackman's costumes showed a kind of a chest-plate armor that looked like a crustacean. Taking off from that very fundamental idea we decided the Cardassians like structure and they'd like to see the structure on the outside instead of hiding it inside the walls. The station itself and all the exterior sets are designed so that you can see the support columns and beams and the skin of the ship applied to the structure rather than the skin covering up the structure as you would in a Beverly Hills mansion."

Although Zimmerman's deconstructionist approach to the architecture of DEEP SPACE NINE was a very different look for TREK, he believes it still is true to the established streamlined look of the TREK universe.

"It's streamlined in a different way," Zimmerman explains. "It's a design that is at the same time honest and a little bit awesome because of the size of the beams that support everything. The size of the windows, the shapes of the doorways, the way the doors operate are all very intimidating. They're not user friendly in the way that the NEXT GENERATION sets are user friendly, and that was intentional. The idea of the creators of the series was that our Starfleet people would never feel exactly at home, they would never be terribly comfortable and always aware it was an alien environment in which they were working."

On Stage 17, in addition to Quark's three story bar and the Promenade, are the sexual holosuites where inhabitants of the station can go to satiate their erotic desires.

"They are like the holodeck of NEXT GENERATION and we can program pretty much any kind of experience for any kind of location we want to. But what we are doing on DEEP SPACE NINE that we weren't able to do on NEXT GENERATION is we see the inside of the holodeck and see the machinery that runs it," says Zimmerman. "When we did NEXT GENERATION we were in a budget constraint that made us do a set that is a wireframe look; it's a grid of squares when the holodeck is not activated and they just see a black void with yellow grids. In the Cardassian holodeck when the lights go off, so to speak, you see the machinery that creates the imagery. It's a step forward for us and it's something we've always wanted to do on NEXT GENERATION and we were never able to achieve."

Director Paul Lynch, who shot "Past Perfect" and "Babel" for DEEP SPACE NINE, and helmed several episodes of NEXT GENERATION, speculates that the holodecks will play an integral part of DEEP SPACE NINE in the future.

"What they will do is what they did on STAR TREK," he says. "On STAR TREK we had alien worlds, but this doesn't go anywhere. This is just what it is here. It has to sustain through drama or through the holodeck sequences and I don't think they're going to have any problems because what is nice is the interplay between the characters. Story aside, production value aside, money aside, I think what people watch when they watch a regular television series is the people and these people are great and I think that's why they're going to want to tune in and watch their adventures each week. I don't think it's going to be a deficiency that we stay in one place."

However, you don't need a holodeck to convince you that the illusions being created on Stage 17 are very convincing.

"You can very much lose yourself into it," says actress Nana Visitor, who plays second-in-command Kira Nerys. "There's that slight edge of insanity--which I don't know if all actors have--where you cross over into the fantasy and you're there and this is really happening. It's very easy to do on DEEP SPACE NINE on these sets."

The ship's interior design is based on the station's exterior aesthetics established by Zimmerman, which exist as four enormous miniatures, the largest being 6' x 6' and used by Visual Effects Supervisor Rob Legato and his team in creating the optical effects.

"The exterior of the miniature of Deep Space Nine is composed of three concentric horizontal rings," details Zimmerman. "The outer ring is a docking ring, the middle ring is an environment and cargo ring and the center ring is the Promenade and the power core of the station. The operations center is on a pedestal that's attached to the center of the power core. The Cardassians like things in three, according to our philosophy, so there are three concentric rings and on the outside ring there are three vertical pylons that are docking pylons. The vertical pylons are also docking positions. At the very end of each of the pylons are weapon banks, phaser and photon torpedo locations, which are arranged mathematically in such a way they make a very pleasing exterior shape seen from a distance. Any fan should be able to recognize the shape of Deep Space Nine the way they recognize the exterior shape of the Enterprise."

Fortunately, due to Paramount's unprecedented success with THE NEXT GENERATION, the studio has been less restrictive on the purse strings in financing the start-up of the new show, allowing Zimmerman and his team the luxury of creating a very exciting visual motif for DEEP SPACE.

"We spent more money on this than we were allowed to spend on STAR TREK VI," says Zimmerman of the set construction budget. "The studio hopes this will be as successful as NEXT GENERATION. The two hour pilot is stunning and it's every bit as good in its way as the original pilot for the original series was back in 1966. 'The Cage' was a brilliant piece of science-fiction work -- especially for when it was done. 'The Emissary' is equally as good."

Unlike NEXT GENERATION which was able to recycle many of the feature film sets (in fact, the Enterprise bridge set on Stage 9 used as the battle bridge in TNG's pilot was first built for the aborted mid-70s TREK TV revival and is the oldest standing set on the Paramount lot), DEEP SPACE NINE started with empty soundstages and a blank slate.

"With the NEXT GENERATION we started out with a lot of feature Enterprise leftovers," says Zimmerman. "We were able to resurrect the corridors which were wonderful and by rebuilding the sickbay we had lots of space to work with. Basically, on NEXT GENERATION the new sets were the bridge, the ops lounge, the crew's quarters and, at the end of the first season, Ten Forward. With DEEP SPACE NINE we started out with a blank sheet of paper. We had three, fairly large empty soundstages and we've filled them with some of the most bizarre scenery that I think the television audience will have seen in a while."

Robert Blackman, who took over as costume designer during STAR TREK's third season, has remained since then. When it came time for Berman to choose a costume designer for DEEP SPACE NINE, he recruited Blackman who will be one of the few NEXT GENERATION crew to do double duty on both series.

"The only thing we use from the features are the Klingons, unless we go back," says Blackman, "We used Scotty's outfit when he did his NEXT GENERATION episode ["Relics"], but we don't use any of that stuff [on a regular basis] because we were trained that it was off limits. What I came up with when we started doing a lot of Vulcans was a look that modified Bob Fletcher's, but it was so complicated that I couldn't get all that Asian look going. I couldn't do it, it was just too complicated, so I found a way to modify it and make it a little bit more of my own elements."

It was Berman who insisted on a new uniform for the DEEP SPACE NINE personnel, rejecting budget-conscious overtures from producer David Livingston who urged retaining the established Starfleet costumes to save money.

"Rick wanted the wardrobe to be new and that was great," says Livingston. "I wanted to use the old stuff, but he said nope, we're going to go for a new look."

Responsible for achieving the new Starfleet look while remaining faithful to the established uniform design was Blackman, whose DEEP SPACE NINE aesthetics went through a number of permutations before producers Berman and Michael Piller settled on a final look for the new outfits.

"The things that are interesting to me are the reversal on the NEXT GENERATION," says Blackman. "Starfleet uniforms have a very dignified and ennobling kind of appearance with that vertical, perfectly done military-esque kind of structure to their outfits. In DEEP SPACE NINE we've taken it in another direction. It's very utilitarian. It's a cross between a NASA jumpsuit and a mechanic's jumpsuit."

Unlike the closely cropped, tight fitting spandex of the NEXT GENERATION's early seasons and the equally padded burgandy and yellow outfits after the uniform's third season refits, the DEEP SPACE NINE uniforms are loose fitting and far less constraining. They do, however, hug the bosom of its leads just as tightly as those on NEXT GENERATION, a STAR TREK staple.

"They're very loose fitting and they have those T-shirts and some people roll up their sleeves so they look like men at work," says Blackman. "I like that notion of a kind of looser and more accessible design. There's something about the dignity which is just wonderful in the NEXT GENERATION, but it's a little bit standoffish. There's a kind of propriety about it and now we've got these guys who kind of open their jackets and their shirts and push their sleeves up and get down to it. It's very hands on existence. It's fascinating to me."

Herman Zimmerman is reluctant to assess his work on the show until the end of the season when he'll finally get a respite from the daily rigors of production. He did, however, take a moment to reflect on his TREK tenure.

"I remember when we finished the pilot of NEXT GENERATION and Mr. Roddenberry said 'People say you can't go home again but we just proved that under the right conditions you can.' I remembered that and that's when I thought that it might be fun to do this without the encumberance and necessary palatte of design criteria that I had to stick to when we designed NEXT GENERATION, and have a whole clean culture and design challenge to just start from scratch. It's been about the hardest thing I've ever done and also the most fun."

Agrees director Paul Lynch, "It's a much more interesting set. This has got so much more going for it. There are so many different things happening on this space station. On STAR TREK the rooms were basically the same each episode; the Captain's quarters, the bridge, the meeting room, the medical bay. Here, because it's such a big space station, there's all sorts of things in it."

"The way the writing is going we're using more sets and smaller sets than I believe they've been doing in stories on NEXT GENERATION," says Zimmerman. "We move around awfully fast for an hour show and it goes very quickly. We have started out with a larger number of standing sets to begin with, but there is no set as big as, for instance, Ten Forward."

One of the most noticeable departures DEEP SPACE NINE has made from established STAR TREK production design is its use of multi-level sets on two of the three soundstages. While the operations center exists on several raised platforms, the Promenade and Quark's bar both are built several stories up. While visually stunning, the set-up creates unique problems for the directors and their craftspeople.

"For a television series, the problems that we've created for the cinematographer are fairly difficult challenges," agrees Zimmerman. "These sets are built more in the nature of the feature sets than the way a television series is generally set."

Supervising Producer David Livingston notes that the use of multi-level sets was not because of space restrictions, but to achieve a new look never before envisioned for the 24th century.

"When we had our initial meetings I pointed out that these sets were wonderful but it would be difficult to shoot," says Livingston. "Ultimately, my recommendation was let's go for it and the directors will just have to figure out how to do it. They cannot shoot the show the same way the NEXT GENERATION is shot. The bridge on the NEXT GENERATION is called the TWA waiting lounge and you can move the camera around with great fluidity and get from point A to point B easily. You can't do that in ops. The Promenade has a whole second story that you have to climb up to shoot on -- but it looks great when you go up there. Quark's bar is certainly not Ten-Forward. It's a lot more complicated and difficult to shoot in. A lot of the sets are smaller and more cramped because that's the nature of the beast here. It does present opportunities and challenges for the director to pull it off in terms of the schedule, but I think it's going to add a visual dynamic that is in strong contrast to NEXT GENERATION."

Director Paul Lynch agrees with Livingston. "The toughest thing always to shoot in STAR TREK was the bridge because it was this big, sprawling space and you had a lot of stuff happening at the back end and the front," says Lynch. "On DEEP SPACE, it's a lot easier in operations because things tend to be more gathered together and you have more elements in the set, so it's more interesting. It gives you a bigger opportunity to do things visually than the control room of the starship. It's more fun and gives you more visual possibilities because there are limitations in STAR TREK with just the sets themselves. Once you've shot the engine room, you've shot the engine room. And I've shot it from just about every angle. Here you've got the main Promenade of the ship with everything from the bar that looks out into the corridors to the corridors that look into the security office. You have a great deal of visual choices, which is neat and more fun."

Lynch readily admits that when he's asked the same question in five years, he may be saying the same things he says about the STAR TREK sets now. "It may well be the same thing," says Lynch. "I'm new here now so it's very exciting because it's all different. We'll see how it goes. I'm very impressed with the amount of money they're spending on the aliens and the special effects. In the two shows I'm doing, there's a lot more effects than anything I've ever done on STAR TREK."

Among the techniques employed to shoot on the treacherous landscape of DEEP SPACE NINE have been the utilization of camera cranes which have infrequently been used on NEXT GENERATION (Rob Bowman, second season on "The Child"; Livingston, fifth season on "Power Play").

"We've used a device where you put the camera on the end of a crane and you put a remote control head onto the camera called a hothead," says Livingston. "The camera operator sits in a chair and is tied by remote control and wire to the camera so the camera is just moving around by itself. That can be used for ops and on the Promenade.

Its use is limited because of the production time it takes to do it. I think you will see a lot more swooping cameras on this show."

Other changes from the standard operating procedure on NEXT GENERATION include an increased reliance on computer generated graphics for scientific and monitor displays.

"When we started NEXT GENERATION the producers were not sure they wanted to use video playback or computer generated images because at that time the state of the art wasn't up to photographing 24 frame film and 30 frame video at the same time. Now we have a very reliable system for reducing video to 24 frames so it can be photographed," says production designer Herman Zimmerman of the myriad monitors that can be found on every set, particularly the operations center which is filled with display screens. "That's a big technical advantage that we've been able to achieve in five years. We have computer generated graphics on video monitors and spent somewhere close to $45,000 just on video monitors for the various sets. I think we have something like 64 video sets in the various places on the three stages."

When STAR TREK: THE NEXT GENERATION was being assembled, Zimmerman recalled Roddenberry's insistence on creating a new viewscreen that would dominate the foreground of the bridge where the images projected on the monitor would dwarf the crew. Used effectively in "Encounter At Farpoint", Picard addresses a menacing Q towering above him on the huge screen. For DEEP SPACE NINE, it was decided that an even more impressive viewscreen would be needed to improve upon THE NEXT GENERATION's advances in much the way that it supplanted the viewscreen of the original series (essentially the equivalent of today's big screen televisions). For the operations center control screen, Zimmerman envisioned a huge monitor that never has an image on it unless it is called up by one of the operations officers.

"There are a lot of things which are new to STAR TREK viewers which we hope they'll like. One of them is the viewscreen," says Zimmerman. "There isn't always a picture of the stars in space as there is on a starship where you can't see the wall through it. There'll be some times when we will be seeing the image on the screen from *behind* the screen. When the viewer is turned off we'll see the image disappear, and the camera will then move in on the people who have been watching it. It's an interesting, rather innovative, photographic technique.

"The effect is done as a burn-in in post-production. Unfortunately, because it's an optical, the viewscreen material can't be pre-produced ahead of shooting because of the way the schedules are so compressed. We're able to cap the viewcreen instead of having it straight up and down, as if you were going to have a projection or a large television screen or a large backlit projection. We put a ring of neon around it and that fuzzes the edge a little bit. We weren't sure if it was going to be an asset or a liability but it turned out to be an asset. It gives the look of the image on the screen a slightly different edge, and that makes it more alien looking. A burn-in on the viewscreen is about the simplest thing we do. We shoot that footage during principal photography and it's inserted in post-production. Although we do call it a blue screen, it's actually green because we're using blue neon surrounding the screen. We use a green saturated color, but you can key off of any saturated color."

In order to realize the alien Cardassian look of the station, Zimmerman was able to construct fiberglass molds which allow him to duplicate panels and features that he wouldn't normally be able to replicate on a limited budget.

"We have created an architecture that will be seen to be unique," says Zimmerman. "We have made all these fantastic shapes in fiberglass and can repeat them fairly inexpensively having made the molds for them."

Another improvement over the familar NEXT GENERATION technology is the use of a turbo-lift on the bridge, which actually can be seen descending and ascending as it transports officers to the heart of the station, the operations center.

"The general consensus was we were competing with ourselves because NEXT GENERATION is a terribly successful show," says Zimmerman. "The idea of STAR TREK is one that has captured the imagination of television audiences all over the world. We had to do something that was at least as interesting and hopefully more interesting. We were intent on making a dynamic place for the operations center. Unlike the bridge of a starship, the operation center doesn't go anywhere. It first orbits a planet and then it's moved near a wormhole.

"One of the things I've always wanted to do was have the turbo lifts actually come into a room and leave a room, and we were able to do that. We only had a certain amount of space under the stage that we could work with so one of the criteria for raising a platform was to gain an extra few feet to operate these elevator mechanisms. We do see the actors come up out of the stage floor and we do see them disappear into the stage floor, and that's very effective. In other sets that isn't possible, so we just see the elevator doors open as we do in NEXT GENERTION. But the Cardassians are a militaristic people and they prefer command from a high point as any general would, so we made the commander's office at the upper level of the operations center. There are windows in the doors, and windows on the sides of the doors and in the commander's office so he can be watching whatever is going on in the operations center. It's a combination of transporter room and engineering area that we would find in another level on the Enterprise. It also has a science area and a large conference room with a planning table."

In addition to the improvement in the new series' production values over its progenitor, DEEP SPACE shows growth over its predecessor in other, less obvious, ways as well. These include its more realistic depiction of women's roles in the future.

Previously, NEXT GENERATION had been criticized for its female roles being too passive and sometimes even sexist. Few would accuse the new show of such a failing.

"Kira makes up for all of that," says Ira Behr. "Enisgn Ro makes up for a lot of it on the THE NEXT GENERATION. Kira is a strong woman and Dax must have a lot of nice conversations with herself. She's a little of everything. We have Keiko and O'Brien aruguing in the pilot about what her role is going to be. She didn't want to come to this station. I think the women are good."

Behr is particularly sensitive to criticism of the depiction of women on the show in light of the complaints levelled about the scene in his fourth season episode "Q-pid" where the men are swasbuckling with swords and Troi and Dr. Crusher hit their antagonists over the head with flower pots. Behr says the scene was devised on the set and was not his doing.

"People might not realize this but even Vash was an attempt to bring in a ballsy woman who's not your typical STAR TREK woman; a clear thinker both in terms of what she did in her own life and sex and the whole bit," says Behr. "There's a lot of talk now about being politically correct and I think more times than not--given this is a show that's in a business that's extremely middle class and conservative and given all those constraints--STAR TREK is fairly politically correct, though that's not something I find really high up on the level."

The strong persona of Kira Nerys was an element about the series that immediately appealed to the actress who plays her, Nana Visitor.

"All I went on was this script I was sent among all the other silly sitcoms and weirdo things of the season, and all I saw was this incredibly strong woman, great writing and emotionally connected scenes I felt I could play very well," says Visitor. "I auditioned, they liked what I did, that was it. Once they gave me the bible they were very available to answer the questions, are we phsyically different than humans? How humanoid are we? For all the questions I had, they had answers. *All* of them. I couldn't catch them on anything. That's all I really required--the backstory of who I am and then basically it's all what makes us tick. It's human relationships and I think that's the strength of STAR TREK. I think we're about human relationships and if Kira changes and grows and learns to adapt and to understand, those are positive messages to be sending out. The fact that she's a strong female is something I don't think is a bad thing to have out there. I'm watching television now and I'm seeing alot of women in very different kinds of roles, in positions of power, and not having to be the sterotypical female and the mom in the sitcom saying 'Honey, get off the couch.'"

For Piller, offering a strong female protagonist was not an answer to criticism of what some have accused as NEXT GENERATION's weak women roles, but a natural outgrowth of the TREK mythos.

"I think we have very strong women on NEXT GENERATION," Piller differs. "They were cast and created as caretaking roles. Their characters are caretakers by their jobs; doctors and therapists are caretakers, and they have a very mothering kind of role. The actors would love to transcend that, but the fact is you have to write the character you've been given by Mr. Roddenberry. As it evolved through the beginnings you have seen stronger and stronger women on the NEXT GENERATION. Ensign Ro is the best example of that I can think of. Tasha was created for NEXT GENERATION, but it was a character that wasn't working and the actor wasn't happy. We went out of our way not to make the women on this [DEEP SPACE] caretakers, although I think Dax is somewhat of a caretaker but she is the science officer so she has a technical expertise to bring to it. There's no question that Kira, or had it been Ro, was always going to be an action hero. You've got scenes in this show where two women are driving a Runabout starship to rescue the male commander who is being held captive. Two women leading a rescue mission. I think we have gone out of the way to create women who are contemporary and really showing us a full range of female experience."

Nana Visitor agrees that it's the positive depiction of women she's pleased with.

"She's a very powerful female and, hopefully, she will be powerful in using what is available to her as a woman as opposed to an Arnold Schwarznegger who wears a little bit of lipstick. She will be affirming for women in that sense, but along with that she's a Bajoran and Bajoran females are very aggressive. She's phsyically trained and was trained as a terrorist. With those female affirming powers she has, she also has what we think of now as male assertive characteristics. She will get into a physical fight. She's not afraid of confrontation. Interestingly, with the ancient Celts the women fought right alongside of the men."

Visitor points to TERMINATOR II as reflecting the continuing evolution of women's action roles, which she feels Kira's persona is an extension of.

"Linda Hamilton was fighting for her child which gives it a strong female impetus," says Visitor. "I think that's the female connection there. There is a powerful reason for force being used and that's very true of my character. There's an emotionally strong bond with Bajor and the importance of the people and the culture and the spirituality being preserved. That's why she can find it in herself to do what she's done and maybe that's the female connection."

In fact, Piller had even considered, in consultation with Rick Berman, making the commander of the space station a woman.

"We sat down and one consideration was that a woman would be Sisko and the star of the show and that, too, would have been an advancement for television," says Piller. "It's not that we didn't take it seriously, we just moved in a different direction because we couldn't put Ensign Ro as commander of the space station. We always figured her as the first officer since she was an ensign."

As STAR TREK fans well know, Michelle Forbes, the actress who portrayed Ro Laren on NEXT GENERATION, was the producer's first choice for the second-in-command of DEEP SPACE NINE. She chose, instead, to pursue a career of features eschewing overtures to join the spin-off. This resulted in Piller and Berman being forced to retool their pilot script to accomodate a new Bajoran officer and second-in-command in "Emissary", the two hour opener that kicked-off the series.

"Michelle Forbes is a wonderful actress and her character of Ensign Ro created the entire canvas for this new series," says Piller of the character he and Rick Berman had created for fifth season's "Ensign Ro", in which the Bajoran Starfleet officer assists Picard in exposing a Federation and Cardassian plot. "It had always been assumed that she would be one of the people spun-off and moved over to the new series. It wasn't part of the plan when she was created. So when we wrote it, we put it together and it would have been fine. Then we showed it to Michelle and she said 'It's a great script, but I really just don't want to commit to a long term deal. I don't want to be in a series.'"

Paramount was reportedly locking their actors into seven year committments for the new series to avoid the costly renegotiations which had resulted when NEXT GENERATION became a smash. Forbes was balking at putting her feature career on hold.

"She didn't really want to be in THE NEXT GENERATION the sixth year either," says Piller of the actress, who will nonetheless remain aboard the Enterprise for several voyages in its sixth season. "She had a feature she had just started and she wants to be a feature actress. She said she would be delighted to be a recurring character, but she didn't want to be a regular. We could not go into the new series that way. For a long time Rick and I talked about seeing if we could talk her into doing a year and we'll kill her at the end of the year. 'If we promise to kill you, will you do it?' But then we decided that we weren't going to have the audience make an emotional investment and then lose her at the end of the year, so we decided after giving her one last chance--on which she passed--to write her out."

Fortunately, Forbes' departure from the series' plans came at the same time Piller was already working on a rewrite of the show to strengthen its first act, which meant changing the character of Ro to another Bajoran with a new and different backstory. This he soon discovered proved an advantage rather than a disadvantage for the new series.

"I found there was a great deal more conflict in having the Bajoran not be Starfleet," says Piller. "Immediately you have different priorities and agendas, and the two people immediately have a conflict with each other the moment they step onto the station. The one between Sisko and Ro would have been a much different one because ultimately she's Starfleet and has to do what the boss says. Kira can do things which are not appropriate Starfleet behavior. We created this character and it was really a matter of rewriting two or three scenes that defined where she was from and a couple of speeches in other scenes which were mostly action type scenes."

Once the character was on the page, it was up to Piller and Berman, with the help of casting director Junie Lowry-Johnson, to bring her to life. After all, Michelle Forbes in only a handful of appearances had become one of THE NEXT GENERATION's most popular characters and would be a hard act to follow.

"We went through a very long casting process and saw some very interesting actresses. Then Nana came in and just nailed it," says Piller. "Bang!"

Visitor, a veteran of a number of television shows including the short-lived WORKING GIRL based on the hit motion picture, confessed to not being an avid STAR TREK fan when she joined the new series.

"I watched STAR TREK when it was in re-runs," she says. "I think I know them all from cooking dinner in my brownstone in New York. I was a fan of the quality of the show, but I was not a Trekkie."

Ironically, Visitor didn't even realize DEEP SPACE NINE was a STAR TREK spin-off when she read for the role.

"I didn't get it and I didn't understand that this was STAR TREK when I auditioned," Visitor explains. "I did not understand what I was getting into. I didn't even know I was wearing a nose [prosthetic] and I talked to Rick Berman He said, 'At least the prosthetic is one of the least we have' and I said 'What prosthetic?' and he said 'It's nothing, it's just a small elephant nose that you wear.' And he had me going for five seconds. But I didn't know, I had no idea. I just knew I wanted to play this woman very badly."

For Visitor, DEEP SPACE is a region of the universe she hopes to be exploring for a long time. "STAR TREK has got so much strength and age behind it and it's cutting edge television," she opines. "We're doing things I've never done or seen on television, and there's this kind of care and the kind of scripts I've never seen. Once in a while I'll have someone I haven't heard from in a year say 'Wow, I hear you're on DEEP SPACE 9, I'm such a Trekkie.' Then I'll say, 'Gee, this is new and different.' I feel that in those very faraway moments on the telephone but in the day to day it doesn't mean a thing except they have the power to allow us to do what we do, and they give us wonderful material to do it with."

CHAPTER THREE
Out of the Cage &
Beyond Farpoint--The Pilot

DEEP SPACE's hefty pricetag--reportedly pegged at between $10 and $12 million--makes it one of the most expensive pilots ever filmed, although many of the costs can be ammortized over the future of its run. This includes the over $2 million spent on the show's sets. By comparison, BATTLESTAR: GALACTICA's three hour premiere in 1978 cost $8 million and BABYLON 5 under $2 million.

Notes Berman, "When you create a premise pilot, which is what we did, you create a two hour show where you have to set up an entire world and an entire group of characters and what brings them together, and at the same time tell an entertaining and meaningful story. You have a big job cut out for you. Mike and I started creating the premise for this show, the backstories for the characters, the relationships they were going to have, and what sort of story would unfold."

The advantage for Berman and Piller was the knowledge gained from over six years of production experience on STAR TREK: THE NEXT GENERATION as well as the lessons learned from producing the first new STAR TREK pilot, "Encounter At Farpoint".

"What 'Farpoint' and five and a half years of STAR TREK did was allow me to know what was possible and what wasn't," says Berman. "What our visual effects guys could give us and what they couldn't. What sets we could expect and how much we could expect to get done and what was pie in the sky."

Berman points out that, as a result, the experience of DEEP SPACE NINE was made considerably easier than when he and STAR TREK creator Gene Roddenberry first sat down to create THE NEXT GENERATION. This also allowed him to avoid many of the ego clashes and production problems that plagued the early start-up of that show.

"Gene had to create a new television show from 25 years of mythology that had grown up over an old one and he had to do it all whole cloth," says Berman of the creation of NEXT GENERATION and the problems inherent on reviving the STAR TREK franchise for television. "In the case of DEEP SPACE NINE, it's much easier for me than it was for Gene with NEXT GENERATION because DEEP SPACE NINE is being produced by mostly people who have been on STAR TREK for five years and understand what it's like to write a stylized 24th century script. [They] know what words can be spoken and what words can't, and how to go about all of the things we do to create this television show as opposed to creating MACGUYVER.

"He also had a lot of people who felt they knew more about STAR TREK than he did. He had to get pretty tough about it and we had a group of writers that came in and didn't have the benefit of someone as strong as Mike Piller. People had no idea what STAR TREK: THE NEXT GENERATION was going to be about. Gene felt the obsessive necessity to put his own print on everything to get the show going, and I applaud him for that. By the time I was sort of in control of the series, in the second year, Gene had pretty much cemented his idea of what the show was going to be about and it was my job to continue, to keep it going and not to formulate it because he had done that."

Some have said that the tone of "Emissary" is far closer to that of "The Cage" than "Encounter At Farpoint", with Sisko encountering a race of aliens who cannot understand linear existence, so they force him to experience his best and worst memories. Once the series premise had been set in place by Berman and Piller, Piller then went to work on writing "Emissary", which would establish the new TREK adventure series.

"I haven't seen 'The Cage' in three to four years, but what brings to mind the memory of it is the imagination that takes you out of that locked cage--Gene's imagination," he says. "It takes you into green fields and the picnic and Susan Oliver and those wonderful moments. I would be lying if I did not say that image was with me when I wrote this script. I don't remember much about it. I don't remember the story, but I remember that friendly green pasture. I think it's definitely inspired by Roddenberry and if people who have missed something in the new STAR TREK feel that some funny bone or some nerve ending is being addressed in the new series, I know Rick and I will be delighted."

Piller points out that he was equally influenced by Roddenberry's "Farpoint" pilot.

"There's a great deal about this structure that's similar to 'Encounter At Farpoint'," says Piller. "One of the tricks I learned from watching 'Farpoint' again was that they didn't introduce Riker and Geordi and Beverly until two or three acts in. I said to Rick [Berman] when we were structuring this, 'Let's hold off the arrival of two of our regulars late enough that I can do something with the other characters.' My first suggestion was everyone was there and they're working and it wasn't as effective."

Ironically, one of "Encounter At Farpoint's" strongest plot elements, the arrival of the menacing Q, was added by Roddenberry to pad out D.C. Fontana's script when he relented to studio demands that the opener clock in at two hours, as opposed to the 90 minute premiere he lobbied for.

"I think the Q thing did come out of a time requirement, but there isn't any question in my mind that the best thing in that show is the Q story," says Piller. "If it had been only that other story it would have been a disappointment. The other thing that comes out of 'Farpoint' is a vision of Roddenberry's where we have Picard arguing for the future of mankind, representing the advocate of humanity to this Q who puts humanity on trial. That's an extraordinary philosphically ambitious idea, and it really helps to define why STAR TREK is what it is. Without that it would have been spaceships and monsters and special effects."

Despite Berman enthusing over the writer's first draft, Piller was unsatisfied with his work.

"Michael's never liked anything he's written," says Berman. "The story was 40 pages long and extremely well defined when Micahel sat down to write the teleplay. He wrote a first draft and then he and I spent about a month working on it. We discussed it, we made changes, draft after draft, and finally we got it to a point where we were pretty happy with it and no one had seen it except for he and me. We had worked on it for a few weeks and he became unhappy. We were looking for a direction and, as is typical to Michael, he was frustrated and felt that something wasn't working. He did a rewrite that was not a major rewrite at all, but it was a rewrite that brought into it the ideas that we had discussed all along that had to do with the Los Angeles riots; the idea of people rebuilding and of people living in an area that had been damaged and that had been violated. And the spirit that goes into the rebuilding of it. It was a good change, but not a major change. More importantly than being a good change, it was a change that made Michael happy."

Incorporating a strong philosphical point of view into DEEP SPACE NINE was of essential important to Piller, whose character of Benjamin Sisko grapples with the alien creatures, actually threatened prophets, inside the Bajoran wormhole to which he tries to explain a linear existence.

"The first day we sat down to meet about this Rick said that somehow this story must have the philosphical ambition that the 'Encounter at Farpoint' script had and that STAR TREK represents," recalls Piller. "Ultimately, what we created was this interaction and confrontation between alien and human that is not so different from 'Encounter at Farpoint', but, of course, on a weekly basis we are exploring issues and philosophies through encounters with aliens. What we have in the pilot is aliens who have no knowledge of a linear existence. What does that mean for Sisko, who is trying to deal with the context of his own personal crisis as it comes out through this philosphical explanation of here's why you don't need to fear me? 'We are not a threat to you and we're different and differences can be good', he says, echoing the same theme that humanity has overcome and we can co-exist in the universe."

The theme of co-existence was amplified by Piller in his second draft when the Los Angeles riots magnified the problem of the divisiveness that existed in our contemporary society. This gave him a new impetus for revising a teleplay he felt was too dull.

"What happened was I had written the first draft of the script, which we had not sent to the studio yet, and Rick read it and alot of people liked it," details Piller. "But something was really bothering me and I couldn't figure out what the devil it was. What it turned out to be was the first hour wasn't good enough. Through the introdution to Sisko we saw things on the station and it scared the hell out of me. When I looked at the second hour of 'Unification', because I'll always consider that a character study of Spock, I realized it was talky and nothing goes on. It's fascinating talk but nothing was happening and I was very unahppy with that. When I looked at this, I was really troubled because I was not falling in love with my own dialogue and my own characters and I was extremely critical. Rick will tell you that throughout this process he has said to me things like it must be terrible waking up every morning and being as negative as you are. But I felt very stongly--and Rick will agree that I dragged him into this rewrite kicking and screaming--that the first hour was flat and that nothing happened and that it was basically dealing out the characters for everyone to see."

Ultimately, what Piller realized was that the characters existed without purpose in his original draft. But with the riots providing a metaphorical iconography for the rewrite, Piller was able to inject new life into the stalled script.

"I said Sisko's not a hero," Piller points out. "Sisko's got to come in and have something to do and have a problem that he has to deal with as a hero. While our mystery is unfolding, which will ultimately blossom in the second hour, Sisko must take this by the hand. In the first draft of the script our guys essentially come to the Beverly Center [a Los Angeles mall] and he decides to stay. I said that's great and the studio said we want to open with a shot of the Promenade and people gambling. So I wrote it that way and I realized it didn't work. Sadly, though, while I was going through this agonzing process, we had the riots in Los Angeles and both of us (Rick was the first to verbalize it) wanted to somehow say there is something to be said in our show about humanity co-existing and coming together. And we want to build this into the alien interaction that we have in the second hour of the script."

Quickly thereafter, the hi-tech DEEP SPACE NINE had been transformed by Piller's pen into a ruined and cannibalized wreck. In Piller's rewrite of the teleplay, he was clearly influenced by the devastation he was witnessing on news reports about Los Angeles on television.

"I had started thinking that it was not a dramatic situation for a man to come to the Beverly Center," says Piller. "It's not very dramatic for someone to go to their favorite mall and decide to stay, but for a man who decides to go to South Central Los Angeles in ruins and decides to stay, *that's* dramatic. In order to bring drama to the first hour I argued with Rick that we should come to a space station that's in ruins and that Sisko must begin the rebuilding process in the first hour in order to be driving the story."

Ironically, what developed out of Piller's new approach to the material was the relationship between Quark and Odo that many of the writers subsequently have glommed onto as the best character dynamic since the bickering between McCoy and Spock in the original STAR TREK.

"We had always had a shape shifting gag for Odo in the end of Act I and we had always had a Ferengi boy, Nog, that would become a friend of Sikso's son," says Piller. "In the rewrite, using all the elements that we had that were waiting to be thrown in, I put Nog at the scene of the crime and put him in trouble. I realized that when Sisko arrives at the scene where Odo is shape shifting--where they meet at the end of Act I--there is this situation where the Ferengi kid is going to jail for being an accomplice to a crime that has been committed. Sisko, who has come to this ruined Promenade, sees the Ferengi guys who used to run the bar and the gambling facilities ready to leave and decides he's going to use this to his advantage."

Sisko threatens to incarcerate Quark, the Ferengi barkeep, unless he stays aboard the station and helps in the re-building process as a "community leader". Despite being repulsed by the idea, Quark is reluctantly forced to stay at Sisko's urging.

"In that scene where Odo is watching Sisko in action and Sisko is doing this number on Quark, I suddenly found myself writing these asides between Odo and Quark," smiles Piller. "Quark is saying, 'What do you want me to stay for?' and Odo says 'I'm a little mystified myself, Commander. The man is a gambler and a thief' and Quark comes back and says 'I am not a thief'. Odo says 'Yes, you are. You're a thief' and suddenly, these guys are going at each other. I realized there's a magic there. There is a relationship there. These two guys have been arch-enemies that have been at each other's throat for the last several years -- and they love it. They get off on this trying to one-up each other, and there's a love that comes within for one another between the good guy and the bad guy that we really explore in the first episode. That's the discovery of character and interaction Rick and I wanted to so much to have. It's a conflict that's fun and restores to STAR TREK something that hasn't really been in evidence since the original show."

Rene Auberjonois, who plays security officer Odo, a shape shifter, and a veteran of television's long-running sitcom BENSON, notes that the chemistry between the cast, both as characters and actors, developed extremely quickly.

"It always amazes me how quickly that happens," says Auberjonois. "You can talk to actors about doing a film and you go on location for 10 weeks and make lifelong friendships, and it's happening here. Because of the nature of the world of DEEP SPACE NINE, which is a space station, there's a sense of community. I have a relationship with Armin Shimerman, who plays Quark the Ferengi, which is very dear to me already. It's sort of a love/hate relationship because our characters are the antithesis of one another. He is a con artist extrordinaire and I am a man who just sees black and white. Something is either just or unjust. It's a very complex relationship and although we're always bickering and I'm always after him, I think we're forging quite a friendship."

"The Ferengi have always, in the past couple of years, seemed to be very broad and on the verge of slapstick," adds Armin Shimerman, the actor personifying Piller's Ferengi con man. "On the other hand, that is how they've been established, so I must include that as well. I don't know what was in their heads about the comic values of myself, but what I think they found in the early episodes is the great comic potential between Odo and Quark. There's this sort of Mutt and Jeff relationship that both Rene and I are savoring a great deal, and I think that's where a lot of the humor is going to come from. Quark is still libidinous, Quark is still avaracious and he's still ambitious and Quark's still short, but I think the humor will come from all those things and his relationships with the humans and the shape shifter."

Writer/producer Ira Behr shared Shimerman's enthusiasm for the developing relationship between Quark and Odo.

"I think Michael and Rick both realized that this is a learning process of finding out together who these people are and then, of course, you cast the goddamn thing and the actors make it who *they* are. Then you sit back and say 'Okay, maybe that's not what I had in mind exactly', but it works and so all the best laid plans of all these things go out the window the second the cameras roll. What I found interesting and fun about this show is not so much each individual character, but how the characters began to interact on the show. Making Odo and Quark this kind of twosome is just going to have juice for ages because Odo is this kind of repressed, haunted figure and Rene's really playing the makeup to a certain extent which is that he's a man alone, which you don't see a lot in the 24th century, and Quark is a Ferengi. He's not your typical cringing Ferengi, he's a Ferengi with a little edge to him. Their comic relationship, I find, is something that's going to be a lot of fun."

But even with Piller's teleplay completed weeks before production began, shooting the pilot was an incredibly arduous affair. It was made more complicated by delays in casting and set construction, which made it arguably an even more difficult shoot than "Encounter At Farpoint" six years earlier.

"I had the same anxieties and hesitations about even wanting to do it because I knew what a struggle it was going to be and the pilot was hard," says producer David Livingston, a veteran of the NEXT GENERATION two-hour opener where he served as unit production manager. "It was hard. Fortunately I didn't have to deal with the day to day minucia of a production manager and I could sort of sit back a little bit. Bob DellaSantina is the wonderful production manager I hired to do this job--just took care of everything for me. It was tough and I told everyone it was going to be tough. It wasn't like just doing another episode or a double episode. It's doing a whole new thing again. It was a pilot and we had all forgotten what that was like. We've had the Life of Riley here for five years and it's all going to change. It was very difficult because there are so many dyamics working; building all these new sets and a whole new cast and new wardrobe. Michael Westmore had to create a bunch of new make-ups, including Odo's, which was very difficult. All of those dyamics made it very, very difficult."

CHAPTER FOUR
The Cast--New Kids on the Block

"Rick discovered Siddig on a PBS show in which he played in the LAWRENCE OF ARABIA prequel, KING FAROUK, and he was very good. Rick said he's great," says Michael Piller. "We'd been looking for Sisko from here to eternity and we told our casting people in Europe to find this fellow. We brought him in and we looked at him and he just jumped off the screen. There wasn't another doctor candidate. He was just delightful. We had not met Avery at that point and we asked ourselves, could Siddig possibly be Sisko? And we found out he was 25 years old and that was too young."

Not since Wil Wheaton prowled the sets of THE NEXT GENERATION first season with gleeful abandon, has STAR TREK been witness to the vibrant and unabashed energy and enthusiasm of a young actor.

Says Berman, "I had seen Siddig on public televison and I sought him out and had the Paramount people in London find him. He is, as time will tell, an extraordinary actor."

It's a testament to STAR TREK's ability to transcend ethnic and racial boundaries that an actor like Siddig could be cast in a role patterned in such a distinctly Michael J. Fox vein. "I read in London with about 30 people," recalls Siddig. "I think they auditioned all over Europe. And then I did one for the big cheeses here. It was bizarre, one day I did the test in London and two days later they asked me to fly to Hollywood where I had never been and, on the same day, they gave me the job which was great."

Unfortunately, as the doctor onboard Deep Space Nine, El Faddil has found himself wrestling with the long-time TREK dilemma of technobabble, the mystical TREK mumbo science that passes for scientific accuracy in depicting a 24th century civilization.

"They have a sadistic love of it," laughs El Faddil. "But I actually quite enjoy it. It's the nearest thing to Shakespeare. Stretching the mind to get your tounge around it and make sense of it, and I actually quite enjoy trying to see if I can make something of it without making it sound flat. That's part of the lie of trying to make it sound like I'm actually a doctor or a science officer. Data on the NEXT GENERATION is an unbelievable robot because he does it flawlessly."

The actor quickly points out that he's not fearful of comparisons with the previous STAR TREK doctors since his character is so dramatically different than either crumudgeonly Dr. McCoy or flightly Dr. Crusher, who have preceeded him.

"I've seen the other shows, but they're such different people than I am," he says. "They've gone for someone younger and he's more naive and not burdened with anything except for the novelty of everything he sees and how best to negotiate it. It completely mirrors my experience. Jumping around and being overenthusiastic comes very naturally to me.

"They're an extraordinary bunch of people," he continues regarding his co-stars. "One of the wonderful things for me being a young guy is, because of the snobby British training I've had, that we're taught no one can act except for the British people. But in this cast everyone has certainly done more Shakespeare than I've ever had hot dinners. They've been there and seen it and have been doing television since they were born. They've got an enromous amount to teach me and I'm just quite happy being at the bottom and holding onto someone's tail. The dynamic, as a cast and as characters, is interesting because it's still developing. We play at games, we go out and have drinks, but I'm still working it out and that's probably my character. I'm the one character who's sitting there watching everybody all the time instead of getting in there and getting my hands dirty."

Also cast early in the process was Rene Auberjonois as enigmatic security chief, Odo. Although viewers may best remember Rene Auberjonois as Clayton Endicott III on the hit ABC series, BENSON, it'd be difficult to recognize him underneath the prosthetic Michael Westmore has designed for him to transform the Emmy and Tony Award winning actor into Odo, a gelationous liquid in his natural shape who has no idea who he is or where he came from.

"Odo, in terms of the kind of person he is and his incredible dignity and sense of justice, is very appealing to me," says Auberjonois. "He's sort of a curmudgeon and he's a very rigid man. He's uptight but he's also got a wonderful deadpan kind of humor. Beyond that he's got a very human kind of pain because he doesn't know who or what he is, so there's this kind of existenstial struggle going on inside of him. He's really just a liquid form. He takes the shape of a humanoid but it's only so he can exist in this world."

As a shape shifter who metamorphsizes into numerous shapes and sizes every episode, the actor is the focus of many of the series state-of-the art visual effects. Since the work is often done in post production, it requires a special discipline to imagine a world of creatures and illusions that doesn't exist until Rob Legato's fertile imagination gets to incorporate them.

"It's the nature of being an actor," says Auberjonois. "For people who are not professional actors, the easiest thing to do is just to remember what it's like to play house. I remember as a kid there was a place in the attic where my brother and I used to go to pretend to be scientists. It's just this willing suspension of disbelief. There's something wonderful about Odo because I turn into all these different things. We shoot things where

I just sort of stand there and I know that I've just turned back from being a rat and it's magical for me to see that."

Portraying Odo is *not* Auberjonois' first foray into the STAR TREK universe. At the request of close friend and director Nicholas Meyer, the actor played the nefarious Colonel West in a sub-plot that had been cut from STAR TREK VI's theatrical release, but restored for its subsequent video edition. In the restored version, the Colonel plots with Klingon conspirators and the Romulan ambassador, Nanclus, to prevent a peace treaty being signed between the Klingons and the Federation. Ultimately, Colonel West is revealed as the man under the Klingon make-up attempting to assassinate the Federation president at the Khitomer Peace Conference.

"I wasn't in STAR TREK VI because the character was cut out," says Auberjonois, who admitted to often being cast as a villain. "I have not seen it. I did it because Nick Meyer is a personal friend and asked me to. I was in Scotland hiking with my wife and rushed back to get the make-up all done. I've played a lot of different kind of parts and I usually play villains and I love them. I remember when my son was much younger and I was doing RICHARD III at the same time I was doing BENSON, he asked why do you always play the bad guy. I said it's because they're usually the best part to play."

However, Auberjonois' Odo is certainly a hero of this series, and he's thrilled to be probing the limits of the final frontier, both literally and figuratively. Odo is the focus of one of the series' earliest episodes, directed by Paul Lynch, "A Man Alone", which addresses predjudice and discrimination. It reflects an evolution for the character that pleases Auberjonois, although even he is not sure what the writers have in store for the mysterious shape-changer in the future.

"It's evolving and there are certain things that I know about him that are clear from the scripts that we've done so far and the bible," says the actor. "The writers know a lot more about where it's going than I do. I like not knowing and opening the script each week and seeing a new facet of the character for me to consider. I like that challenge each week. It keeps it fresh for me, which is very important when you're doing a week-in and week-out schedule and watching the character develop like this. When you're doing a series, the characters always develop to a degree, but I think in this kind of situation, more than a sitcom, where the characters really are cast and you know what's going to happen, there's a certain wisdom revealed in the character. He has an incredible intelligence in one episode, and in another there's a weaknes in his character that's revealed, a rigidity he has to work through, a human quality which is very interesting."

Also pleasing to Auberjonois are the interrelationships developing with the other characters on the show.

"There's something specific with every other character," he says. "My relationship with Nana Visitor, who plays Major Kira Nerys, is a very interesting one because she is above me in rank and yet she comes to me for a certain kind of wisdom. I'm very interested in seeing how that develops. For me, the mystery of who he is is going to be is the thing that keeps me plugged into the character. In a way, I hope it takes a long, long time to figure out who he is. I don't mean to be pollyanish about it, but I'm just so happy with the character and the stories that we've had to do. Ask me that question in a couple of years, maybe I'll be a jerk, but right now I'm just in here plugging and loving every minute of it."

Nana Visitor plays Nerys, the aggressive second-in-command and a former Bajoran terrorist. Visitor, a veteran of a number of television show's including the short-lived motion picture-inspired WORKING GIRL, confessed to not being an avid STAR TREK fan when she joined the new series. "I watched STAR TREK when it was in re-runs," she says. "I think I know them all cooking dinner in my brownstone in New York. I was a fan of the quality of the show, but I was not a Trekkie."

Visitor's hopes for the character reflect the inner passions felt by Kira, whose loyalty to her people and homeworld motivate her actions.

"My hope is that Kira may change from this course of being someone who isn't necessarily always right and who has a button pushing relationship with Sisko," she offers. "They just set each other off in a certain way, but she's growing and changing. In our second episode, she opens up to Odo and asks for help with her problems. I get to do it all. I hope it stays this way. I love the physical stuff and that she's running a ship and waging war."

The one aspect of the production that Visitor, who recently had a baby, finds warying are the long hours required to shoot the show.

"They're long days," she says. "And that's something we're all finding our sea legs with--16 hour days. I have a six month old baby and I'm just figuring out how to see him and do this. It's not impossible, but you have to be more creative. My husband brings him at lunch sometimes and I feed him Gerber and then it's kind of interesting to go and yell at Sisko and then come back and say 'Come on, it's apricots and tampioca'."

For Visitor, DEEP SPACE is a region of the universe she hopes to be exploring for a long time.

"STAR TREK has got so much strength and age behind it and it's cutting edge television," says Visitor. "We're doing things I've never done or seen on television and there's this kind of care and these kind of scripts I've never seen. Once in a while I'll have someone I haven't heard from in a year say 'Wow, I hear you're on DEEP SPACE 9, I'm such a Trekkie,' and then I'll say, 'Gee, this is new and different'. I feel that in those very faraway moments on the telephone, but in the day to day it doesn't mean a thing except they have the power to allow us to do what we do and they give us wonderful material to do it with."

Also cast early in the process was Armin Shimerman, who plays the Ferengi Quark, a veteran of several NEXT GENERATION episodes. Having pioneered the weasley role of a Ferengi in the first season NEXT GENERATION episode introducing the race, "The Last Outpost", Shimmerman was a natural choice for the role.

The co-star of such series as BROOKLYN BRIDGE and BEAUTY & THE BEAST, Shimerman has also appeared in the films BLIND DATE, LIKE FATHER, LIKE SON and DEATH WARRANT. The actor is quick to contrast his new character of Quark with previous Ferengi incarnations, who many dismissed as an inept attempt by TREK to find a new adversary for the Federation during its early evolution. Shimerman attributed his casting to his previous outings as a Ferengi on the series and felt he could best personify the new Ferengi character they had created for DEEP SPACE.

"They remembered me from five years ago as one of the first Ferengi," says Shimerman. "I think what Rick said to me was they remembered how strong a Ferengi I was because they wanted that for Quark. He also has to be able to play chess with Sisko. They wanted that quality. I did not have to audition as many times for a series regular as I would if they had not seen my work and were keeping me in mind. The first time that I had a callback, and usually there are a number of actors sitting there, it was only me and Max Grodenchik. He's played a Ferengi before. At the final audition, it was just me. They gave me the impression after I was cast that they had indeed written the part with me in mind."

Shimerman admits to a degree of frustration about working under the huge prosthetic appliance that covers his face, but laughs that, unlike Levar Burton, at least he can use his eyes. "I think every actor would prefer if all of his face was shown," says Shimerman. "I would be a fool to say otherwise, but I think the mask works really well and the combination of the mask and whatever inflections I can give to my voice and my eyes comes across quite well.

It means working a little harder and being a little bit bigger. I'm used to playing roles where its very low-key and underplayed. I've been trying to teach myself to do that for years. Now, all of the sudden, I'm being asked to overplay a little. It's just a new challenge."

Although most of the cast was lined up before production began, late casting of the role of Benjamin and Jake Sisko, as well as that of Dax, weeks into shooting on the pilot, made it an extremely difficult shoot for the department heads.

"They cast early, but we couldn't get them until one week before the show started shooting," says costume designer Robert Blackman. "The principals arrived pretty much at the same time, but for an episode where there was a lot for them to do and a lot of multiple costumes, it was difficult. Sisko had six or seven outfits to wear in the pilot. As we get a board with a shooting schedule saying the first week you'll be shooting this and the second you'll be shooting this and the third....and so on, that's how we build, in that kind of order since everything is made to order. We had a lot of the background costumes started but the shooting schedule started changing when they didn't have Dax cast. The more they would pull stuff up from the fifth week of shooting and stick it into the first week, the more you're completely unprepared. It was amazing, but we pulled it off."

With most of the cast in place, the impending commencement of principal photography on August 18th made the casting search a race against the clock. It was imperative that Sisko and Dax be cast before photography began on the pilot.

"It's an ugly business and its interminible and it's exhausting," says Rick Berman. "We have a wonderful casting director [Junie Lowry-Johnson C.S.A.] and we just began the process. I think that Rene Auberjonois is a remarkable actor, I think Nana is remarkable and my favorite on STAR TREK since the beginning has been Colm Meaney. I adore Colm's work."

Colm Meaney has served aboard the Enterprise since it's first encounter at Farpoint, although most fans won't remember it since he was a nameless face on the battle bridge. Since then, through sheer charisma, the actor has elevated himself from an anoymous transporter chief to the only married recurring character on THE NEXT GENERATION. Now he is a co-star aboard DEEP SPACE NINE.

"I was in New York for a year with BREAKING THE CODE and that was the year of the writer's strike. STAR TREK didn't get going again until September or October," recalls Meaney of his return to NEXT GENERATION after having shot the pilot. "When I came back, they brought me on as Chief O'Brien. For the first five or six shows that I did, he just kept cropping up and I was Transporter Chief. Then, a script arrived and suddenly he had a name."

Meaney has kept busy on the silver screen as well as the small screen, starring for Alan Parker in THE COMMITMENTS as a reverent fan of Elvis; a malevolent terrorist in UNDER SIEGE, and a fighting Irishman in Ron Howard's FAR & AWAY. During his treks away from the decks of the Enterprise, the actor has also appeared as the ill-fated captain of a 747 in DIE HARD II: DIE HARDER, a cop in DICK TRACY, and Dennis Quaid's brother in Alan Parker's COME SEE THE PARADISE. Surprisingly, Meaney agreed to join the cast of DEEP SPACE NINE when he was approached by Producers Rick Berman and Michael Piller to become a regular on the new series.

"We knew we wanted to do something with O'Brien who we brought over to the show," says writer/producer Ira Behr. "Colm is a really fine actor and he's had limited chances on THE NEXT GENERATION. This year he's a lead and we're trying to find different and new things to do with him. One of the things we're going to do is team him up with Bashir in a certain way. Bashir sees O'Brien as kind of the old pro from Dover, the guy who's done it all. The way I see O'Brien is as the working man's hero, and so does Bashir. He wants to be like him and wants to know him and emulate him. O'Brien looks at this young kid from the Academy with that English, upper class accent and it's like, 'Go away, kid, you bother me.' It could be fun because you don't usually see that. We shot a scene where Bashir is talking, talking, talking and he turns to O'Brien and says something to O'Brien. He just gives Bashir a look, with not one line of dialogue, that's like 'Get the fuck away from me kid'. It's funny, it's good and it's character."

Meaney agrees that O'Brien has sort of become the everyman of STAR TREK.

"O'Brien is somebody who is more human," says Meaney. "He obviously likes his job, but he also has other aspects to his personality. He doesn't have the element of being a fearless super human. There are situations they get into which, because of their Starfleet training, they react to as if it's normal, with steely nerves and all that, but I think O'Brien doesn't like that stuff too much."

Berman says of the rest of the cast, "Armin Shimerman, who has worked with us, we brought in on Quark, having been on NEXT GENERATION three different times, and he's just an actor who I've always respected. He came in to read for Quark and just nailed it. So with Colm Meaney and Siddig [El Faddil, Dr. Bashir] and Rene and Nana Visitor and Armin we had a core of five remarkable actors. It finally came down to our star and the role of Dax, which were the two killers."

The search for Sisko was the first one to be filled only days before production began, prompting Avery Brooks to reportedly pronounce, "This is the role of my career." Piller and Berman had even toyed with casting El Faddil as Sisko after Berman discovered him in a PBS telefilm and arranged to put him on tape in England. When the two producers realized the actor was only 25 years old at the time, they knew they would need to look elsewhere for Sisko and finally found Avery Brooks who, in addition to touring in a play about the life of Paul Robeson, is best known as Hawk from ABC'S SPENSER: FOR HIRE and the short-lived spin-off, A MAN CALLED HAWK.

"Patrick Stewart has a very big pair of shoes to fill and we needed to find someone who was different but had the same stature and the same strength and power," says Rick Berman. "It was a very, very long search. We brought people from Belgium, we brought people from England, we saw German actors, English actors, we saw a lot of American actors, black actors, white actors, Hispanic actors and we finally chose Avery Brooks who was undoubtedly the best. But it was a very, very long process."

When seeing Avery Brooks attempting to order a cup of coffee from the operations room's replicator, he's almost unrecognizable. The menacing, morally ambiguous strongman of ABC's SPENSER: FOR HIRE and A MAN CALLED HAWK, was sporting a full head of hair and was considerably subdued compared to the in-your-face attitude he had displayed in both series as Hawk. However, once Brooks opens his mouth, it's immediately clear that the producers of DEEP SPACE NINE have found a fitting successor to William Shatner and Patrick Stewart as the latest actor to personify the lead of the newest STAR TREK series. He conveys not only the power and strength of a Starfleet commander, but also the emotional depth and complexity that have endeared both previous captains to two generations of television viewers.

When Stewart and Shatner were cast, both, despite an impressive array of supporting credits, were not as well known as Avery Brooks. Brooks had created a very recognizable visual icon during his three years playing Hawk, but Executive Producer Rick Berman didn't feel his lack of anonymity was a liability in casting him for the role of Sisko.

"He played the second role on a show and it did not last a long time," says Berman. "There are actors I tend to stay away from because I feel they have overly familiar faces. But to me a good actor is somebody you don't think about how familiar they are. If they're right, they're right."

Despite early rumors, denied by Michael Piller, that Richard Dean Anderson of MACGYVER was a front-runner for the coveted role of Sisko, Brooks was chosen days before the beginning of principal photography on the pilot. Ironically, Brooks played his best known role bald and the question remained, in light of Patrick Stewart's well-noted baldness, would Brooks continue the tradition?

"We think he looks best with hair," says Producer David Livingston. "In fact, we looked at several variations of hair and we felt the one we chose was the most appealing and the way he looked best. It was simply a cosmetic decision and had no bearing on Patrick Stewart."

Like Stewart, Brooks commands an instant respect on the set from his fellow actors and will no doubt prove to be not only a role model for people of all races, but will write a new chapter for the advancement and depiction of blacks on television, continuing to take STAR TREK boldly where no conventional series has gone before.

For Brooks, DEEP SPACE's allegorical approach to addressing contemporary issues is a refreshing change from the mundane fare offered on network television, reflected in the fact that he portrays a single parent. This, he feels, illustrates the show's topicality in addressing 90's concerns within the framework of future society.

"We're dealing with a single parent and single parenting," says Brooks. "In the last twenty years there's a very different notion in our society and, indeed, our world about what that means, so of course in an allegorical way this show is very 90's. We're on the verge of the 21st century and then it will be very teens. Teens in the 21st century."

Equally difficult was the casting of the science-officer. Piller and Berman were ultimately drawn to the race of the Trill, which existed as a joined species as first examined in NEXT GENERATION's "The Host", in which an alien ambassador who is having an affair with Dr. Crusher is discovered to be a parasite which exists within the body of a host carrier.

"Originally, we had the science officer in a a wheelchair since she came from a planet with different gravity," says Piller. "Eventually Ro befriended her and finds her a gravity free environment on the station where she could fly around. Out of her office she would be in a wheelchair, which was necessary for her to move around. Although a character like this could possibly show up in the future, production requirements made her untenable on a regular basis. So we looked at a variety of other alien species and, of them, the Trill seemed the most interesting."

The Trill of DEEP SPACE NINE now exists within the body of a 28 year old female who knew Sisko in its previous body, that of an old man, creating a fascinating dramatic and comic relationship between Dax and Commander Sisko.

The search for the woman who could portray the Trill was the most arduous one, and when the producers finally decided on Terry Farrell [HELLRAISER III] they were already weeks into production on the pilot.

"I was stressed to death," admits Farrell of being the last actor to join the cast. "They did all my stuff in one week and I had the flu and my period and 16 hour days and a big lump on my forehead that we reshot for two days."

"The most difficult role to cast is always a beautiful girl," says Executive Producer Rick Berman. "Beautiful women are few and far between and to find one who can act and who doesn't want to bypass television to go into the movies, is very difficult since there are very few of them. Fortunately, we finally found Terri."

Of the casting process, Farrell adds, "It's so overwhelming. I'm so glad it's over. It's so incredible getting STAR TREK anyway because it's such a legend. In August when I first got it, it was like a rollercoaster ride that I couldn't get off of and you don't know what's going to happen."

Rick Berman admits that part of the difficulty of casting the role was the problems they had in explaining the part to those auditioning. "It was very difficult to say you're a beautiful woman and a 400 year old androgynous character at the same time."

Recalls Co-Executive Producer and Co-Creator Michael Piller, "We were already in production when we cast Terry and part of the reason that it's so difficult to cast is because it's a character that's a little harder to define. I could write a book about Trills now, but what does that mean in the day to day existence of these people? How do we make it different from Terry Farrell? How do you make it something alien and yet accessible? It's a very interesting mix of qualities that I think the studio wanted. Rick and

I felt that we wanted a woman who was attractive and yet a superior actress. We saw a lot of very talented young women, but they just didn't get it. Some would change their voices, to make it sound like a man's voice coming out of a woman. It was hard. The casting people will tell you that the roles of people 25-35, attractive and brainy are the hardest roles to cast in television. It's hard to find the next Meryl Streep. It's hard to find the next Glenn Close."

Fortunately, Terry Farrell, who had recently finished work on the Tony Hickox film HELLRAISER III, was called in by Junie Lowry to audition.

"Terry came in the last day or two of casting for this show and wc had hcr back a couple of times," says Piller. "We had two or three others that we were very interested in, but truth is Terry was the only actress who came in to read where Rick and I looked at each other and agreed that she had hit the scenes that she was reading. We had finally got to the place where we *had* to cast somebody. Terry did not have the experience of some of the others, and we knew, and she knows, that there was a great challenge of acting and performance ahead of her. So far it's amazing to watch her, because you can see a much stronger performance. She's starting to grow more and find this role."

Farrell agrees and says the key to her audition was playing the role with an amused detachment as opposed to attempting to personify a woman with a "short, fat snake inside."

"I think she has fun with people," says Farrell. "In the scene I had to audition in I said I used to be an old man and Avery expects to see him in that context. He had never seen me before as a woman, so how else do you play that other than to have fun with somebody? It would be fun if you dressed up in make-up and the other person doesn't know you're fooling them and they're trying to believe you're who they say you are, but you don't look anything like you did last week. Just having fun with it was the key for me."

Preparation Farrell *didn't* make for the role was boning up on her science.

"In biology I did really well, I got straight A's, but this is different," says Farrell. "I'm not the doctor! You just open the writer's guide and I call and ask Michael Piller, who's really nice if you have a question about the technical jargon. Sometimes they write a question mark where the 'tech' should be and you wonder what's going to be the word there. Cough it up! I know they're going to freak me out and then I end up getting something like 'the ionic L-band emission patterns don't match'. I'm supposed to know this by heart? Tech with a quesiton mark? I'm getting more used to it now. That's what really upset me during the pilot because I didn't even know where to start. What am I talking about? I'd try to relate it to a car and it wasn't working."

After Paramount executives reviewed the dailies on the pilot, they issued one of their few ultimatums. The distingushing marks on Farrell's forehead, denoting her as a

Trill (as actor Franc Luz had worn in "The Host" as Odan) had to go. After the protracted search for a beautiful actress who could also act, the studio didn't want her to be defaced by prosthetics.

"There are different Klingons and now there are different Trills," jokes Farrell. "Maybe I'm from the north of Trill and the other guy was from the South."

With the ensemble finally in place, principal photography on "Emissary" was completed with rewrites coming in from Piller at the same time that some of the sets were still being completed. However, the biggest obstacle to the fledgling series had been overcome.

Herman Zimmerman suggests that the new STAR TREK ensemble is more faithful to Roddenberry's original hopes for STAR TREK before the casting of William Shatner and Leonard Nimoy turned the show into a star vehicle.

"If you want to go back to Mr. Roddenberry's original ideas, he wanted to create an ensemble cast and he did, but because of the really strong ability of Bill Shatner and Leonard Nimoy and the romance of those characters and the relationships between each other and Dr. McCoy, it became more of a star cast than an ensemble cast. In NEXT GENERATION Gene achieved what he was really striving for in the first place. He has the strengh of Picard in Patrick Stewart, but he has a very level competent cast all the way through. I think he was more pleased than he was the first time around with the casting of NEXT GENERATION."

Avery Brooks admits to an instant affinity for the material. "I'm new to it," says Brooks. "Of course, I was familar with it because I grew up watching television, but I am definitely a fan now."

Producer David Livingston offers that while the new TREK carries forward the progressive traditions of color-blind casting established in the original STAR TREK--which put black, Asian and Russian characters in lead roles--there was no intent to be politically correct in casting a black actor as the lead and other minorities in important supporting roles.

"We got the best actors for the parts," says Livingston. "STAR TREK is about the fact that it doesn't matter what you look like or what your skin color is or if you have weird bumps on your head or stuff hanging out of your ears or weird colored hair or a mishapen body. It doesn't matter in the 24th century. People don't deal with that anymore. First of all, you're exposed to so many bizarre, different kind of people, who has time for prejudice? It's silly, it's an outmoded kind of thinking and that's a credit to Gene and to Rick and Michael to continue that point of view. One of the key characters on this show is a Ferengi, and of all the creatures we've had, they're probably the most unappealing types. Yet now that they're part of it."

"The only role that was ethnically locked was we wanted Sisko and his son to be the same race," says Berman. "We read people, black and white, for every role. In the case of Cirroc, who plays Sisko's son, he is half Ethiopian, his mother is Ethiopian; and Siddig is half Sudanese, so we have two actors who, on one side, are from Northeast Africa which is very interesting."

Michael Piller agrees, "We were definitely looking for the best actors for the roles. And if the best actor for the role had been Asian, you would have had an Asian commander. We were faced right from the beginning with the challenge of making this show unique and different and a step beyond THE NEXT GENERATION. The last thing we didn't want to do was be accused of simply doing another STAR TREK and exploiting the formula. Rick and I had a very high ambition to contribute to television, to not just put another quality hour on the air, but to try and advance television in our own way. We're very inspired by Gene, and Gene advanced television. We can't hope to do that in the same manner that he did because he was there first in the pioneer days.

"The ground has been broken," he continues, "but I think so much of television rests on its laurels or looks backwards or tries to find what works, what's safe. There has never been an hour dramatic series that has had a black lead that was successful. The old boys network in the television community would tell you that it's a huge risk to put a black man in the lead because it will turn off a certain segment of your audience. Rick and I felt right from the beginning that we wanted the opportunity to consider a black lead for this show. We were delighted and impressed when the people at Paramount allowed us to have a full range of auditions to consider all races and all people. When it got down to it, we were delighted that Avery Brooks turned out to be the best actor we could find. We knew the pundits would tell us it was a risk, but if there was any franchise on television that could support this risk it would be STAR TREK and we felt we might be doing a little something for television."

CHAPTER FIVE
Deep Space Illustrations

If it's true that, despite the adage to the contrary, books tend to get judged primarily by their covers, it follows that if DEEP SPACE NINE makes a favorable first impression on viewers, a large portion of the credit for the show's video "cover" is due to Ricardo Delgado, the illustrator who storyboarded the series' main title sequence.

"Every week for at least the next season, the first images you'll see on the show were designed by me for Dan Curry, the visual effects supervisor for the title sequence," Delgado says. "To me it's an homage to both shows, the original series and THE NEXT GENERATION. It opens up with a starfield, which will immediately harken back to the first series. There'll be a lot of beauty passes with planets as well as cool-looking passes over the station, which is an homage to the dry-dock sequence in STAR TREK: THE MOTION PICTURE. I was sitting in the theater watching that film, and everyone else thought the sequence was going on so long, panning over the ship, and I thought, that's cool, look at all those spotlights. We all owe the initial series all the respect that it deserves. It was my way to hook up all three shows. I remember listening to Herman [Zimmerman, the production designer] saying 'Space, the final frontier,' is what got you from out of the bedroom to get your ass in the living room to watch some cool TV. It was important for me to do that, to get that from the original series, this from the feature films and that, the planetary passes, from THE NEXT GENERATION, and amalgamate them all to one hopefully cool-looking main title sequence."

Delgado's contributions as illustrator on DEEP SPACE NINE do not stop with the opening of the show. Along with senior illustrator Rick Sternbach, who holds that position on both STAR TREK series, Delgado is responsible for a large portion of the pre-production drawings that become blueprints for a wide variety of elements on the show.

"I've designed everything from matte paintings to ships to interiors of ships, etc." points out Delgado. "I sit down and have fun all day. My day-to-day responsibilities could be anything from helping the graphics department put some graphics in to designing the starships. It runs the gamut. Sometimes they'll need a prop designed in two hours. You're under the gun, and that becomes a challenge to your sense of design. That's the best part of the job. The writers write it, and have a certain way that they visualize it, but the rest is up to us. It's the best of both worlds."

Between the two of them, Delgado and Sternbach design all of the major elements required by a given script.

"We'll both read the script and we will come up with our own ideas," explains Delgado. "During the production meetings, they decide which direction to go in. We both have a distinct way of thinking. Rick's genius is that he's very knowledgeable in the technical aspects of the show, having written the Technical Manual [along with Michael Okuda], whereas my imagination seems to run all over the place, so we get really good concepts from both of us. A lot of the time we'll come up with two concepts that will be amalgamated into one. In that sense everything is circular on the show. Rick will often go to the extra effort of designing things that have not been assigned to either of us, basically improving the show."

The design of the Deep Space Nine station itself, as realized in the enormous six-foot in diameter model that was built as the primary miniature for the series, represents for Delgado the best example of the inter-departmental cooperation that is his favorite aspect of working on the show. "The model is a wonderful amalgamation of everyone in the art department, not just Rick and me, but Michael Okuda contributed, Doug Drexler and Denise [Okuda], and they have come up with a graphic style that was incorporated into the exterior of the show, as well as two of our set designers, Nathan Crowley and Joe Hodges."

"The basic configuration [of the station] was from Herman's idea, and everyone extrapolated from that," he adds. "Nathan Crowley and Joe Hodges set the standard for Cardassian architecture, which is a wonderful mixture of pseudo-fascist and crustacean. You'll get a giggle hearing it, but hopefully when you see the show, you'll see that the exterior of the station is a carapace. The way we thought of it was that the Cardassians are really bad guys, so fascist architecture, real serious, dark, was called for. It's like looking at an insect. There's a shell on top of it, and if you pull off the outer shell, there're some really cool intestines on the inside of the insect, and that's where Mike [Okuda], Doug Drexler and Denise Okuda come in. They do some really wonderful graphics and bring those 'intestines' out and give them a really unique quality. Rick came up with some really interesting ideas for the center core of the station."

Although DEEP SPACE NINE is set in the same universe, the fact that the station's architecture was Cardassian rather than human-influenced set up a challenge for the DEEP SPACE NINE art department.

"The two directions we had to go in," notes Delgado, "is that we knew we were part of a time-honored history of design, and yet we knew that we were also establishing a new sense of direction. The fact that we were both honoring Federation design and coming up with our own gave us a great deal of range to come up with designs. Coming up with a distinct look, while retaining the aspect of STAR TREK was the best part of the job."

Delgado's goal was to create a look distinct enough from that of THE NEXT GENERATION that viewers would come to associate it with DEEP SPACE NINE as much as the Federation look has come to evoke its sister series.

"The way I looked at it," says Delgado, "is that if you turned on the show halfway through the hour, you would know whether you were watching NEXT GENERATION or DEEP SPACE NINE. I think we successfully solved that challenge. The Federation look is sleek and sharp and glossy. That standard was set way back in the Sixties. You'll look at our show and immediately know that you're not watching NEXT GENERATION. There'll be some Federation elements, but the whole space station is of alien design, not Federation."

Despite the fact that DEEP SPACE NINE has a different overall look from THE NEXT GENERATION, it is still very much a STAR TREK series. Delgado, who is only three years out of art school and, despite his many accomplishments in the short time since then, still considers himself a bit wet behind the ears, was initially a bit apprehensive to find himself one of only two members of the DEEP SPACE NINE art department who had not worked in some capacity on THE NEXT GENERATION.

"I walked in, and Michael Okuda and Rick along with Andy Probert had been there since the beginning," explains Delgado. "I felt a little awed, because you go all the way back to Matt Jeffries, the original art director. He designed the Enterprise. Those guys weren't slouches at all, they were great art directors, and I was just coming in and hoping to do my best and to fit in. Thankfully, everyone's been receptive to my work. I really appreciate that. My concern was the STAR TREK universe and how we would all fit in there, and so far it's been great."

One of the reasons Delgado had such an easy time assimilating was his prior familiarity with the work of two of his colleagues, Sternbach and Okuda.

"It was easy to fit in," he admits, "because of the pioneering work Mike and Rick had done, and because of the Technical Manual. You could be anywhere in the country and you could pick up a Technical Manual and in a month you'd have Federation inside and out. That's the brilliance of their work. We owe a great debt to them because they made it easy to walk in. You pick up the book, you read, and you know what they're doing."

More than once on the show, Delgado has turned to the Technical Manual when faced with designing a new incarnation of an already-established technology.

"When we designed the replicators on the show, we wanted a distinct look," he says. "So I looked up what the replicators are doing in the Technical Manual and I started from there. It's basically a ground work. Having established that, it made our job a lot easier."

Although he came to DEEP SPACE NINE with a fan's knowledge of the prior series, Delgado considers his relative lack of experience with the STAR TREK universe to be a strength, insofar that it allows him to approach design problems with a non-Federation influenced eye that is rare in an art department comprised of STAR TREK veterans.

"I sit down and look at what has already been done, let's say for a ship design," Delgado proposes. "I try to go in a different direction from something that's already been done. We don't always want to see a cone or an X-wing type of structure. I come up with a couple of different sketches of different concepts. I'll do a three-quarter front, a rear, and a bottom view, and that should be pretty much enough. Then, if Herman and the set designers like it, it goes out. If it's a ship, it goes out to the model builder. I'll just hand it to him and say, 'Here are the drawings, now have fun with it. Do something really cool.' Then it's up to them to come through with it. They'll even come up with a lot of extra stuff on the model itself and make it look wonderful. I can only contribute a certain amount of blueprints and reference materials, then after that it's up to the guy who builds the model. It's hard for me to be disappointed, because I'm such a fan. If you put a ship up there in front of a blue screen, and you light it, hey, that's fun for me."

Delgado found that the experience of designing a show on a weekly basis was substantially different from designing the series pilot.

"For the pilot we had more time, obviously," he says. "We knew that we were designing something that was going to be built [to last] for at least five years, and that can affect your thinking, from designing the starship to designing graphics for the sickbay, not just because it was built to last, but because you knew that this stuff really had to sing when it was on screen. You knew that the bar had to be a really great bar, because it was going to be there for how many years, how many episodes a season? That was foremost in our minds.

"Now that we're in the episodes, the important thing is serving the script, and we obviously have less time than we did for the pilot. We try to read the script as soon as possible, extrapolate different concepts, run them by Herman, and get them approved or disapproved. We're working at a faster pace, but actually, it's more fun. There's more ingenuity involved. With the Promenade, I knew that I had a month or two to come up with different concepts. All I did for several weeks was do different shop fronts, different interiors, different concepts that were used or not used for different reasons. Now, if there's a shop that has to be designed, they need to have the sketch within a couple of days. Sometimes there'll be an existing set and we'll have to change it around. You have to think quicker. You have to think on your feet and see one thing in something else. To a certain extent, I think that's in a different way more fun than the pilot, because we're running and having a good time."

Delgado, who cited the French artist Moëbius as the primary influence on his drawing style, singled out certain elements of the shoe as those he was most satisfied with.

"I'm most proud of the interior of the ship. That's very important to me, because when you sit down and think about it, you're setting a design standard for a show for the next five years and beyond. People around the world are going to see the model for Deep Space Nine, and I can say I helped design that model. I'm proud of that.

"I'm also proud of the operations center, Ops. That's a really cool bridge. I don't know how anyone can be disappointed walking onto that set. You're expecting the bridge of the Enterprise, and you don't get that at all. Boy, that thing is big.

"The third thing is the Promenade. To my knowledge, that has to be the largest set ever constructed for television. Walking through and seeing all the shops, the bar, the VersaTeller is really enjoyable. A little bit of trivia is that I came up with the sketch for the VersaTeller on the Promenade, and they built the thing. That was great, seeing something that wasn't in the script but I sketched out, and the next thing you know, it's lit and a Ferengi bank is running it, and there's all kinds of logos on it, including a Romulan logo. You see the characters walk by it, and if you don't see it right away, it's okay, because I know it's there, and now readers will know it's there.

"I also designed the Cardassian bed that appears in the pilot. I imagined the Cardassians would probably move up officerwise through political assassination, so I designed the bed with a force field around it when you sleep. When you walk up to it, you step on the off button, and the force field comes off. Then you lie down and step on the button and the force field comes on again. The interior is not designed yet, but I would think you have a monitor to watch the latest video or whatever, and you can sleep peacefully knowing you're not going to get a knife in your chest. That was something that I enjoyed.

"I had a big hand in the Promenade. The café was an initial sketch of mine extrapolated by Alan Kay, one of the set designers. In my initial sketch there was an alien plant that undulates through the latticework on top, and I was glad to see that they followed that pretty closely.

"One time, I did a sketch of the interior of a shop, I won't say which one, I'll leave it up to the readers to figure out. I took it to Herman, and he said, 'Boy, that's cool.' Then he turned it upside-down and said, 'I like it better,' so they built it that way. Now, more often than not, Herman will turn my sketches upside-down before he approves them. I don't know if that's good or not.

"We spent three or four months building the Promenade, but it's not until you put smoke on the set, put people in front of the camera and aliens around it that it comes to life. Then you believe you're on a space station. You take it for granted that the whole thing exists. The whole show coming to life is the best part of it for me. I'm just glad I'm along for the ride.

"I'm following a lineage of great designers. I'm just a young buck. I come in to a show on a daily basis, and I design things that billions of people are going to see. That's something that takes your breath away."

And the challenge of creating an actual look for the show was somewhat breathtaking for the rest of DEEP SPACE NINE's crew as well.

"We're moving significantly away from the Starfleet look that we've established for the past five years," observes NEXT GENERATION scenic art supervisor Michael Okuda, who was a chief architect of the Starfleet look.

When Okuda agreed to do double duty by accepting the same position on the new series, he entered a fresh corner of the STAR TREK universe.

"Because Deep Space Nine is essentially a Cardassian facility, we're having a lot of fun coming up with a new look, new technology, new architectural details, new control panel layouts, new styles of readouts," says Okuda. "That's a great challenge. A lot of it is essentially trying to come up with familiar things, but doing it in unfamiliar ways. For example, control panels, the format for the buttons on the control panels. We have very specific styles for the movie Starfleet, and very specific styles for THE NEXT GENERATION Starfleet. Doug Drexler and I have come up with some very bizarre styles of keyboards and button layouts which we hope look functional, but we also hope they look very different from what you've seen in the previous versions of STAR TREK, as well as in other movies."

"Despite the fact that the two facilities, the Enterprise and Deep Space Nine, were theoretically built by completely different cultures and are very different technologies," Okuda explains, "the fact is that they're both made in the present day on planet Earth at a film studio using present day technology. Hence the technologies used to create both looks are very similar. It's only in the artistry, in the design and execution, that they become different."

"Cardassians have a lot more [console displays] that are based on a radial design, outward-flowing displays. Theirs is a much more graphic-oriented technology. They have relatively small amounts of text or symbology. Hopefully the information comes from the design, as opposed to Starfleet, which has an enormous amount of text and statistical tabular information [in their readouts]."

One of the elements of design used to visually differentiate the Cardassian look of Deep Space Nine from the Starfleet look of the Enterprise was color. Herman Zimmerman's overall production design clothed the sets in darker colors than are seen on THE NEXT GENERATION, primarily grays and blacks, with gold highlights. For their part, Okuda's team also used a separate and distinct range of colors for the control panels on Deep Space Nine.

"We have a very specific color range that we use for Starfleet," says Okuda. "We have a separate and distinctly different color range for the Cardassians, as well as a third distinctly different color range for the STAR TREK feature films. The features tend toward cool blues and greens. THE NEXT GENERATION tends toward an interesting pastel range of oranges, purples and mauves. The Cardassians' is an interesting color mix. Even though we're using very similar techniques to create a control panel [for both series], the fact that the designs are different, and that they're very distinctly different color ranges, will hopefully create a different look on film."

During previous seasons, when he only had THE NEXT GENERATION to contend with, Okuda was able to do much of the hands-on work of designing the control panel displays. In fact, he was so instrumental in creating the unique look of the readouts on the Enterprise that the cast and crew began referring to them as Okudagrams, a term that the characteristically modest Okuda himself never uses.

Now that Okuda is responsible for the graphics on two major weekly science fiction series, he has had to delegate much of the design work.

"It has diminished my hands-on involvement with both shows. The studio asked me to take a more supervisory role with the graphics," Okuda details. "Because I have two strong teams on both shows, I can just pop in to offer guidance and try not to make their lives too miserable."

In practical terms, this has meant that Okuda devotes most of his hands-on attention to designing the images that will appear on video monitors, leaving the design of the control panels to his assistants, Doug Drexler and Denise Okuda (who also happens to be his wife). Drexler designs the layout of the control panels on a Macintosh. The layouts are then made into large format lithographs which Denise "colorizes" by cutting out colored gels and gluing them to different sections of the lithographs.

One of the most impressive results of Denise's color work is the enormous simulated stained-glass window panel that stretches the entire height of Quark's, Deep Space Nine's Ferengi bar. This piece presented Denise with a particular challenge because it was made from a relatively small lithograph that was enlarged to many times its original size. This meant that even a tiny flaw the size of a human hair would be visible when the piece was blown up to full size. It was a tribute to Denise Okuda's skills with the gels that the final result, which serves as the visual centerpiece of the bar, displays no such defects.

It is somewhat ironic that Okuda is spending so much of his time working with video monitor displays on Deep Space Nine in light of the fact that one of his major innovations when he began work on THE NEXT GENERATION was in developing methods of creating moving readout images that could be accomplished without the more expensive video monitors. Okuda perfected the polar motion gag, in which the illusion of motion is created in an image by rotating a piece of polarized material in front of a polarized illustration.

It was by coming up with clever solutions like the polar motion effect that Okuda developed a reputation for being able to achieve impressive visual display effects without requiring the set to be equipped with expensive video monitors. That is why it is ironic that, because he demonstrated so successfully that it was possible to create great animated readout screens without expensive live video monitors, the producers developed so much faith in him and his potential to do impressive things with DEEP SPACE NINE that they sprang for the expense of installing actual video monitors all over the space station. Thus by showing that he could get along without video monitors, Okuda was eventually given those monitors to work with.

"The fact that in five years I've generated probably hundreds of pieces of animation for THE NEXT GENERATION for its post-production readouts gave me the confidence," says Okuda, "and it gave the producers the confidence to say, 'OK, we can do this, it's not a big unknown, it's not a huge risk.' [As a result,] when you look at our sets, if you look at the operations center, the instrumentation is more alive."

Despite the fact that he has now delegated a sizable portion of his work load to his assistants, Okuda nonetheless has his hands full to overflowing with the responsibility of doing both STAR TREK series simultaneously, and he is still learning just how to accomplish that feat.

"We're still relatively early in the production cycle with DEEP SPACE NINE," he says. "A lot of things are still nebulous, we're still discovering what the show is about in a lot of ways. With each additional show we learn more about better ways to do things and we get a better idea of what the producers expect of our work. I imagine there'll be a fair amount of evolving between now and the end of the season."

Okuda's day-to-day schedule doesn't leave him much time to catch his breath.

"Generally we get a script approximately seven working days prior to the beginning of an episode," he details, "so we have seven days to design and prepare everything. On the seventh day we start shooting. Doug and Denise will work with the set designers as well as our production designer to anticipate as much as possible what's going to happen. The challenge with all this, of course, is that the script is constantly evolving as the preparation goes on. They'll be adding sets, they'll be changing sets, the director will suddenly decide that he or she wants a particular kind of shot, so the set will change accordingly. Then, on the seventh day we start shooting for seven to eight working days. During those seven to eight shooting days we are prepping the following episode.

"Approximately two or three weeks later, I'll get a rough cut of an episode and I'll start working with the post-production department to prepare animated graphics for burn-ins." These burn-ins are the animated screen displays that were not actually playing on monitors during shooting but must be added optically as a post-production visual effect.

"Now, simultaneously, of course," says Okuda, "I am working with the production designer, Richard James, on THE NEXT GENERATION, and I am doing exactly the same thing with the art department there, so it's an interesting juggling act."

Surprisingly, Okuda has no difficulty jumping from THE NEXT GENERATION to DEEP SPACE NINE and back. "I did the same thing during STAR TREKs 5 and 6," Okuda explains, "working on both projects. It's actually kind of fun to be in Cardassian mode and then in Starfleet mode, to go back and forth."

CHAPTER SIX
Michael Westmore--
Make-Up Maestro

Michael Westmore, who has won the Emmy more than once for his makeup designs on THE NEXT GENERATION, is one of a handful of STAR TREK staffers who now find themselves pulling a double shift, performing the same duties on both STAR TREK series. In Westmore's case, serving as makeup supervisor and creator of both THE NEXT GENERATION and DEEP SPACE NINE has more than doubled an already considerable workload.

"There isn't any difference in the job," Westmore observes of his responsibilities for the new series. "It just doubles the job. We're still doing the same types of things."

Actually, the work has *more* than doubled. Because Deep Space Nine serves as an interstellar crossroads visited by a wide variety of different races, each episode is populated by a significantly larger number of aliens of a wider variety of races than was the norm on THE NEXT GENERATION, as the Enterprise is a ship primarily run by humans with the odd alien crew member or visitor popping up in relatively limited numbers.

"Instead of having a guest alien coming through NEXT GENERATION, which we've had now and then on the show, on the new show I have them every week," explains Westmore. "Aliens on DEEP SPACE NINE is a way of life, it's expected."

Aside from the simple fact that there will be many more of them, the aliens of DEEP SPACE NINE will not differ markedly in conception from those that appear on THE NEXT GENERATION.

"It's the same time period," says Westmore. "We will run into some similar aliens on both shows, because this isn't a million light years away. The Enterprise docked there in the pilot, and Patrick was in there for a while, and Colm Meaney has transferred off the ship and is there as one of the organizers. So I will have a crossover of aliens. Instead of having two separate shows, the two shows tie together, and we can do that very easily through my department by bringing a feel of the same creatures. Each show will have it's own individual new ones that will come into it, but as far as background creatures, we have, for example, the Bolin, the character who plays the barber on THE NEXT GENERATION. You will see that same race in the Promenade on DEEP SPACE, so we know that there isn't just one of these things out there, that there is a race of these people. There's one in the DEEP SPACE pilot. He's an officer in the opening sequences, and now we have a female one who has been seen in the Promenade walking around. We're able to tie that particular alien race up and weave it between both shows. I've done that with several others. There was another alien, a bald orange creature with a turkey throat and a spoon nose called a Rotciv that I put together just to walk down the Promenade. It turned out to be so interesting that we put him in a little teeny bar on NEXT GENERATION, and now we have him back in the Promenade again."

The area of Deep Space Nine where the widest variety of aliens are to be glimpsed at any given time is the Promenade, a large, multi-level shopping mall-like area that has no real equivalent on the Enterprise.

"We've got our bar, Whoopi's little Ten-Forward," says Westmore, by way of comparison. "We have had the occasional alien or Vulcan in Ten-Forward, but it's mainly been human that we've had in there. Over on DEEP SPACE NINE, the space station is actually run by Bajorans, so we have a big mixture of Bajorans, and that means having to apply a nosepiece to all these people and having many more aliens."

"We also have a Ferengi bar, Quark's," he continues. "It's managed and run by Quark, who's a Ferengi, and he's got a Ferengi bartender in there working for him. Then whenever we step out into the promenade of the space station there has to be a mixture of aliens out there from all over the galaxy. On every show that we've done so far, every time we go into those areas, I have had to have a complement of aliens walking up and down with the Bajorans and the humans."

Although many of the alien creatures are background characters, glimpsed only briefly and often from as distance as they quickly stroll past the camera in corridors or on the promenade, Westmore has made it a point of pride to shun the practice of saving time and money by not putting as much detail into the makeup of the background characters as that of the principals. Although Westmore knows that the attention he pays to making up the background aliens is missed by most viewers, he takes satisfaction in the knowledge that there is a core of dedicated fans who take note of even the smallest details of his work.

"Almost ninety-nine percent of the fan letters I get," Westmore points out, "are thanking me for the quality of the show, that you can watch the show, and you don't see a Halloween mask, or where obvious lines are where this thing has just been slipped on, or where the colors are different. It's literally motion picture quality. I think that's part of why I survived there for so long. I brought my motion picture experience into it, and I won't settle for any less than that."

In fact, Westmore's high standards are well-known at Paramount. Although it is rare that something will go so wrong with makeup that Westmore's temper will begin to peek through his otherwise disarming demeanor, the event is not unknown.

"If I go on the set and I see something wrong, I have been known to go crazy," he admits. The worst incident of this nature occurred last year during the filming of the NEXT GENERATION episode entitled "Ethics," in which Worf's spine is operated upon to cure paralysis. Westmore had devoted considerable time and attention to creating a very realistic Klingon spine for the scenes in which Worf's entire spine is removed from his body. Unfortunately, prior to shooting those scenes, the prosthetic spine was unintentionally bent into an arc position rather than the spinal position in which Westmore had originally sculpted the piece. By the time Westmore got to the set and discovered the error, it was too late, the master scene establishing the position of the spine had already been shot. Westmore was so incensed by the error that, by his own admission, he temporarily lost it "very violently." After he had some time to calm down, he was able to view the event with a bit of perspective.

"The thing was, nobody ever really noticed the error," reflects Westmore. "But I had in my mind the way it should be. After you spend so much time building something, you expect it to be perfect when it goes on camera. I can blame it on myself, because the person who put it in there didn't know what was in my mind. I should have been there. I should have taken just a minute and gotten over there to double-check it before it went. It just makes me want to be able to double-check on everything before it goes. It was like a little reminder that I've got to keep on top of everything."

Now that he has two shows to keep an eye on, Westmore is faced with the difficult situation that twice as many things have the potential to go wrong, while he has even less time to check on individual elements.

"Things do slip by once in a while," he concedes. "Especially now. I can't be everywhere at the same time. I have to try to rely on the best help that I can hire to be my extensions. Then I try to get around to everywhere to make sure that something doesn't go wrong and slip through the cracks. But it's Murphy's Law."

Westmore does hire a large number of experienced makeup artists to help him turn out the required quota of aliens. In addition to his permanent staff of four assistants on DEEP SPACE NINE, which is separate from his staff of assistants on THE NEXT GENERATION (and includes Jana Philips, daughter of Fred Philips, original makeup artist on the classic series), Westmore hires a varying number of additional freelance makeup artists on a day to day basis, the number hired determined by a particular day's workload.

"I hire a lot of people," Westmore says. "When I say a lot, I'm talking about maybe ten extra makeup artists for the day, every day. I sit down in my office with the call sheet, and I'll make a list of all the characters that need to get made up and who has been making people up so far, then I add the makeup artists I need to finish out the morning to the list. I call it the battle plan. I may need five makeup artists at 4:30 in the morning, and then I may need another three makeup artists at 5:45. I just lay all this out and then go over it with Production to explain what my needs are to be able to supply them with the talent at a specific time, knowing that some makeup is going to take two hours, another one may take three-and-a-half and something else might only take an hour to do. I have to juggle this every day on both shows."

One thing Westmore does not have to worry about is a shortage of freelance makeup artists willing to work on the show at a moment's notice.

"I have Oscar winners that are working for me," smiles Westmore. "People enjoy coming over. These top-quality makeup artists enjoy coming over and working on STAR TREK because it's fun. In between features they come over and give me a hand."

Although all of his assistants are experienced makeup artists, those that are new to the particulars of applying Westmore's unique makeup designs do require Westmore to come in a little earlier in the day than he would otherwise have to in order to provide extra guidance during their initial period with the show.

"I have to keep an eye on them that first day and work with them," he explains. "We've been going through a lot of artists lately on both sides of the street, both shows, and for the first few days I had to go in there and watch them to make sure that the shoulders got centered in the right spot, that the earlobes got centered in the right area, that they lined up in the jawline with the chin and that the nosepieces got on straight. Then, after a couple of days, I might not have to go in at 4:00 in the morning, I might be able to go in at 6:00, just when everything is winding up, and check it out before it goes on camera. I have to rely on the older ones and myself to check the new people that are coming in as we're going along."

Westmore's concerns about the new makeup artists are not entirely unfounded. Although rare, there have been incidents that justify the extra attention.

"One morning we were doing Vulcans," recalls Westmore. "I passed the ears out to everybody and I said, 'Put the ears on and make sure the points go straight up. I don't want them tilting forward or backward, the points should go straight up over the center of the ear.' Everybody glued their ears on. All of a sudden, this one guy goes walking by me, and he looks like Mercury, the ears are actually pointing toward the back of his head. The makeup artist had put the right ear on the left and the left ear on the right and then had painted them in. Everybody else was walking around with Spock-directed ears and this guy, they were going backwards. All he needed was the helmet. It was funny because it was correctable quickly. Most of the time mistakes like that are tragic at the moment - you need to correct it as quickly as you can. But the Mercury ears on that Vulcan, that was too much. We all had to sit down and laugh at that one."

Even with the extra hired help, working on two major weekly science fiction series doesn't leave Westmore with a surplus of free time. How much of his time is taken up by the two shows?

"I'll let you ask my wife that," Westmore laughs. "She never sees me. I have to take the earliest call on whatever show is coming in early. And one of them is always in

Avery Brooks as Commander Benjamin Sisko (photo © A. Berliner/Gamma Liaison)

Nana Visitor as former Bajoran terrorist and current Deep Space Nine First Officer, Major Kira Nerys (photo © Celebrity Photo Agency)

Rene Auberjonois as Deep Space Nine's shape-shifting security chief, Odo (photo © A. Berliner/ Gamma Liaison)

Terry Farrell as Trill Science Officer Jadzia Dax (photo © A. Berliner/ Gamma Liaison)

Armin Shimerman as the Ferengi Quark (photo © Celebrity Photo Agency)

Siddig El Faddil as Chief Medical Officer Dr. Julian Bashir (photo ©
A. Berliner/ Gamma Liaison)

Colm Meaney switches over from Next Generation as Chief Operations Officer Miles O'Brien (photo © A. Berliner/ Gamma Liaison)

Cirroc Lofton as Benjamin Sisko's son, Jake (photo © Celebrity Photo Agency)

Three of the heroes of Babylon 5 pause for a behind-the-scenes candid shot (photo © Cinemaker Press)

Top: Patricia Talman as Lyta and Andreas Katsulas as G'Kar getting along better than anyone would expect (photo © Cinemaker Press)
Bottom: The Babylon 5 space station (photo © Warner Bros.)

Commander Sinclair and Security Chief Garibaldi walk the main corridor of Babylon 5 (photo © Warner Bros.)

Top to Bottom: Cast members of Babylon 5 and Space Rangers preparing for action (photos respectively © Warner Bros. and Trilogy Entertainment)

Jeff Kaake as Boon, lead hero of the Space Rangers (photo © Trilogy Entertainment)

A variety of Michael Westmore alien creations for the Deep Space Nine pilot, "The Emissary" (photo © David Strick/ Onyx)

Make-up maestro Michael Westmore displays Data's head as seen in Next Generation's "Time's Arrow" (photo courtesy David Ian Solter)

*Two behind-the-scenes moments during the making of "The Emissary."
Top: An alien brunch courtesy of Michael Westmore; Bottom: Nana
Visitor loses it on the set while an amused Colm Meaney looks on
(photos © David Strick/ Onyx)*

Jan. 2-8

TV GUIDE

89¢

SCI-FI ISSUE

STAR TREK'S
NEWEST FRONTIER
DEEP SPACE NINE

Bill Bixby
fights for his life

Long Island Lolita
One crime,
three TV movies

Charles & Di
Sneak peek
at the movie

0 1

0 864415 2

Avery
Brooks
and
Patrick
Stewart

EXCLUSIVE PHOTOS

1ST EPISODE
PLOT SECRETS

SPECIAL TO TVG:
CAPT. PICARD
BRIDGES THE NEXT
GENERATION GAP

PLUS Babylon 5
and TV's Sci-Fi Boom

Avery Brooks and Patrick Stewart as Commander Sisko and Captain Picard adorn the cover of the January 2-8th 1993 edition of TV Guide (© Murdoch Magazines) early. It is very commonplace now that I have to get up at 4:00 in the morning and go into the studio. I try to get out of there sometime between 7:00 and 9:00 at night to be able to get back in again at 4:00 the next morning. They had to put a beeper on me. There are about a dozen places that I could be at any one time, so the only way to find me is to beep me instead of trying to call all the phone numbers where I could be."

Westmore has hopes that eventually things will fall into more of a routine and his schedule won't be quite as grueling as it is now.

"It'll settle down as it goes along," Westmore says hopefully. "With DEEP SPACE just starting off, there's a lot of organization that has to be done, a new crew to get together. Eventually we'll get the system working like the well-oiled machine NEXT GENERATION has become."

The large number of aliens created for both shows requires an equally large supply of the basic tools of Westmore's trade.

"The amount of supplies," he observes "it's a quantity that's mind-boggling. I go through over a ton of plaster a year and I don't know how many gallons of latex. I buy latex five gallons at a time. I did buy a fifty-gallon drum once, and we used that up, but we had to keep stirring it so the solids wouldn't separate, and it got to be a pain, so it was easier to go back to using five gallons at a time. I'm buying a five gallon drum every other week."

That's substantially more than the four to five hundred pounds of plaster and the ten to fifteen gallons of latex he used to create the makeup for MASK, a relatively makeup-heavy feature.

"I have a room at the studio where we store the molds," says Westmore. "There's probably five tons of plaster molds in there from the last five years. I'm talking about foreheads, noses, cheeks and hands, not full bodies. This is all tied up in all these little mini-molds."

Whereas in previous seasons all of the mold-making work was done in one lab, Westmore has now divided the work for both shows between two different labs.

"Our old lab is where we do our mold-making and our rubber work," Westmore explains. "I now have an upstairs lab that's close to the NEXT GENERATION trailer where we do sculpting and painting. This way I'm able to use the same help. If all of a sudden things are slow on one show I can move the help, bring them across the street for painting or helping with gluing."

In his six years on STAR TREK, Westmore has created so many alien races that he and his crew need to make up descriptive nicknames for each creature in order to be able to identify them.

"The first season I could tell you every name of every character and what they looked like," says Westmore. "Now, just to be able to conjure up the creature, we call them names like Cauliflower-Head, Fish-Face or Tiger-Man, using some characteristic of the creature. It's easier for us to remember those than a lot of the alien names that are put to them."

Back when he only had one series to contend with, Westmore designed aliens to order, creating races as new scripts called for them. The increased demand for aliens has caused Westmore to change the pace at which he designs creatures.

"Now, with DEEP SPACE going on, I'm not even waiting around for scripts anymore," he explains. "In fact, I've got two aliens in clay now that there's no parts for, no nothing. I'm going to go ahead and design these things and probably put them into DEEP SPACE. Then if they like it and a principal character comes along, we'll resurrect it and build it for the principal person. But I'm going to have a background person now, just so we don't wind up with the same things all the time, so we always have fresh things going."

Once he had begun designing creatures on his own schedule without always waiting for a script to require one, Westmore briefly toyed with the idea of putting aside his best designs until there was a script that could use them for the principal characters, but he soon realized the creative pitfalls of that approach.

"I'll come up with an idea and say, gee, that's really a good idea. I think I'll save that," Westmore details. "But I've found that if I try doing that, then the next time I try to design a character, I am aware that it's my second choice, and I don't like to do that. So now, if I come up with an idea, I go with it. I figure, if that's the furthest that my imagination's going to be able to stretch, I'm going to be in deep trouble. So if I come up with an idea and go with it, then when a principal comes along, I will design something new or design something that's on a similar basis. Maybe by designing that first one, and being totally satisfied with it after building it, applying it and coloring it, I will say to myself, gee, if I had made the cheek here a little longer, it would be interesting, or if I put the bumps going this direction, it will give it a different feel. I learn things from that one to apply to another one that's coming along."

Aside from the many Bajorans that are seen each episode, there are a number of recurring characters that required more extensive makeup designs, a task initially made particularly challenging by the unusually short lead time between the actors being cast and the commencement of principal photography on the DEEP SPACE NINE pilot.

"We didn't have a lot of time up front to do a lot of makeup tests," Westmore explains. "Because the actors were not cast that far in advance, we were not able to do a lot of testing and throwing-out and re-testing. We had to get in and really burn the midnight oil to get the faces done, get one little test in, maybe make a minor adjustment, and go with it, go real fast."

Among the major recurring makeups were Odo, the shape shifter. Although the actual shape shifting effect is done with computer animation in a variation of the popular morphing technique, Westmore had to design a look for the creature in its natural state.

"The whole front of his face is an appliance that gives him a   very textureless, plastic look," says Westmore. Dax, a recurring Trill on DEEP SPACE NINE, underwent a change from the Trills seen on THE NEXT GENERATION.

"The original Trills on NEXT GENERATION had a forehead on and a little nosepiece," Westmore points out. "They decided to change that, they wanted a different look to the character, so I do a spotting on her. I have to personally do it by hand every day. It starts up at the top of her forehead, comes down around her hairline, in front of her ear and down the sides of her neck. In the pilot, she's even lying on a table, bare to the top of her bustline, and I had to continue the spots down her body. It's a laborious job, but there seems to be no easy way to make a stencil up for that, it just has to be hand-done every day."

Another heavily made-up character is Quark, the Ferengi owner of the bar that bears his name.

"He has a nephew by the name of Nog," says Westmore. "He's a Ferengi teenager. We've had some fun with him. To give him a younger look his base is a little lighter, and we put freckles on him."

Of all of his designs so far for DEEP SPACE NINE, Westmore is most proud of a character named Tosk he created for an episode titled "Captive Pursuit."

"The scale system on his body is based on an alligator," he notes. "It's a scaly skin structure that's over all exposed skin. His sleeves are rolled up to his elbows, so his arms are scaly all the way up that high. We've got hands on him, a full head. I made a small set of dentures that go in his mouth, not to give him fangs, but to break up his nice tooth line, and he's wearing contact lenses. It works really well, the way the rubber fits his face, around his head, and the way he twists his neck. He's able to put the stuff on and forget that he's in rubber. He's able to perform as if this was what he really looked like."

Ironically, this, the favorite of Westmore's designs for the show so far, was produced under a schedule so tight that it would seem to mitigate against good results from any less-talented makeup artist.

"The first rubber was run on Wednesday," says Westmore, explaining the tight schedule within which he is often forced to work. "The second head that we were able to use came out on Thursday. I started to paint it Thursday night at 6:00 and finished painting it at 9:00. We were back in at 5:00 Friday morning, and the head was still wet. It was so fresh there was moisture inside the rubber head. We stuck it in the wig oven for a little bit just to dry it out. The rubber still wasn't fully dried-out when we put it on the actor and he went on the set to work. That's the time frame that I am under. That's what I enjoy about the show - that we don't have tons of time. But the character turned out to be gorgeous."

Despite the wide variety of aliens Westmore has designed for both series over the past six years, there are those who have accused him of a lack of originality due to the generally humanoid shape of his creations, not understanding the restrictions under which he labors.

"I still have to go back and live with Gene Roddenberry's original concepts," Westmore explains. "Rick Berman still goes along with those too. I got a call from an outfit in Santa Barbara that wanted to offer me some STAR WARS-type creatures that they'd designed and wanted to see on STAR TREK. I explained that we have a Gene Roddenberry concept that we have to live with, and that's why so many of our creatures walk like a human even though their faces are different. We run into a lot of humanoid races where they're mainly different forehead designs, but that is the concept of the show. It's not that we couldn't do something else, but we're being true to an original idea."

Westmore feels that the only reason the same complaint wasn't leveled more frequently at the classic series was that it wasn't on long enough for the basic humanoid pattern of the aliens to be as easily discernible.

"This show's going on longer and longer," he emphasizes. "The original show only went on for three seasons, and you could do a lot in that time. We're just going on a long time, so we have to keep coming up with something. I still don't think we have duplicated anything in the six years."

Westmore is aware that the humanoid nature of the aliens is more of a concern to STAR TREK fans than to general viewers, but he also feels that such fans are understanding when he explains the situation to them.

"Not everybody sits down and watches every single show," says Westmore, "but I do, and there're some Trekkies who do too. I go to the conventions, and when that's explained to people, that this is what our policy is, it's understandable, especially when you say, 'It was Gene's idea, it's not my idea.' This is what he wanted to tie the universe together. He wasn't really making wild and crazy science fiction films. We deal with real problems and 'real' aliens and 'real' humanoids by leaving this piece of humanity in them that we can associate with as a person, instead of having a giant claw. Every once in a while, we'll wind up going to the holodeck and doing something that's a teeny bit different. On an episode of NEXT GENERATION this season called 'Schisms' we put some very long claw-like pincers on an alien race that abducted Jonathan [Frakes], but it doesn't happen that often. Once in a while we're able to slip it in."

CHAPTER SEVEN
F/X On DS9

Most people would say that, with a diameter of over one mile, the space station known as Deep Space Nine is quite large.

"It's huge," agrees Rob Legato, although he's actually speaking of the Deep Space Nine model, which though much smaller than the object it portrays, is still at six-feet in diameter a giant among miniatures.

Legato, the visual effects producer on STAR TREK: DEEP SPACE NINE, is well aware of the requirements of miniature effects photography, having served as visual effects coordinator, along with Dan Curry, on the first five seasons of THE NEXT GENERATION before taking over the reigns on the new series. His extensive experience with shooting the Enterprise models allowed him to suggest a few modifications to the design of the Deep Space Nine model. It was a miniature Legato wanted to ensure was as easy to shoot as possible, considering that, if all went well, he would become intimately familiar with every curve and cranny of the model over the run of the series.

The producers came to Legato with the art department's original design for the spherical station.

"We didn't change too much," says Legato. "The producers and designers had something very specific in mind in terms of what they wanted to do. There were just a couple of things [that we suggested changing], just to facilitate shooting it. It was actually a very good design, a terrific design that's very interesting to photograph. It's fun to shoot because there are so many great angles on it. It really begs for motion, going past beams and various structures. Even pushing in a foot will make it look like you've traveled a tremendous distance. There was nothing that really needed to be added to make it better."

The most important suggestion Legato had for the final model concerned its size. The design of the station, a central core surrounded by thin radiating arms, presented a unique challenge for the visual effects team. If the overall station were built to be the same size as the Enterprise model (about four feet in diameter), a size that is normally very convenient for the effects team to work with, the core of the station would be significantly smaller. It fact it would be too small to easily work with, the result of what Legato calls "negative space," the relatively large amount of empty space between the core and the arms of the station. At the other end of the size spectrum, if the model were made large enough for the central core to be a comfortable four feet in diameter, then the radiating arms would stick out so far that there wouldn't be enough space in the room for the motion control camera to get far enough back to shoot the entire model. Thus, the six-foot diameter size was arrived at as a practical compromise between the conflicting needs of the effects team to have a model large enough to easily maneuver around and shoot, and a model small enough to fit in the motion control room.

"It was as large as we can make it and still shoot it, and as small as we can handle," Legato confirms. "If we make it any larger we just can't shoot it, because now the whole model is too big, and if we made it any smaller then we couldn't shoot the middle part because it would just be too small. We found a comfortable size that we can deal with."

Legato also had some say in the color that the model of the station was painted. "The paint scheme that they originally came up with, the colors were so dark that they would go black, so we backed off some of those and made them a little lighter in tone. Some things you think you'll get on film, you don't. If a tone is too subtle, it looks good to your eye, but then when you photograph it, it goes away, especially on television. The darker you make a ship, the more difficult it is to light, and then there's a tendency to over-light it. Experience says you have to back off on some of that. We added some external lights to the ship to spotlight certain areas which also give the illusion that it's much larger than it is."

Although Legato now praises the originality of the station's design, there was a brief period when he thought the design would have to be fundamentally altered for a very simple practical reason: he couldn't figure out a way to mount the model. Normally, a model of the ship is mounted from below on a pole which is then optically matted out in a variation on the blue-screen process to create the illusion that there is nothing supporting the ship. The problem with mounting the Deep Space Nine model was caused by the thin arms that extend above and below the core of the station. If the model were mounted in the traditional way, on a pole attached to the bottom of the core, the number of angles from which the model could have been photographed would have been severely limited. Even though the pole itself would have been matted out, as the camera moved around the model, the pole would have the rear arms of the station as they were eclipsed by the pole, thus destroying the illusion that the station was free-floating in space.

The solution that was eventually arrived at was to reinforce the station's arms so that they were strong enough to support the weight of the entire model, and then to mount the miniature on a plate attached to the bottom of the reinforced arms, thus eliminating the need for a pole entirely while mounting the model from its lowest point rather than the bottom of the core. Legato doesn't know the identity of the person responsible for this new method of mounting the model, but he is certain the innovative idea came from someone who wasn't bound by an over-familiarity with standard visual effects techniques.

"I think it was somebody in the art department who came up with the idea," Legato speculates, "somebody who doesn't normally mount these things. It's probably the best way, because they saw it with a fresh eye. They don't know from tradition. They don't know what normally is done."

In order to eliminate elements from the frame that would detract from the illusion of reality, like the plate on which the model is mounted, Legato employs an orange screen rather than the more widely-used blue screen. The model is shot in front of a large screen made of an orange material that glows bright orange when lit by ultraviolet light. The mounting plate is covered with the same material. Once the camera movements for a particular shot have been determined and programmed in to the motion control computer, the model is shot a number of times, with the motion-control rig upon which the camera is mounted precisely duplicating the same move on each pass. During one of these shots, the matte pass, the model is illuminated with ultraviolet light, causing the orange material to glow brightly. The sole purpose of the matte pass is to record on film a very clear, bright image of precisely those elements in the frame that should not appear in the final image. Ironically, in order for these undesirable elements to be invisible in the completed effect, it is necessary for them to be the only visible elements during the matte pass. The image resulting from the matte pass is then used to create a matte that blocks out only those elements that were glowing, the mounting plate and the backdrop, from the final image. Legato prefers the fluorescent orange screen to the traditional blue screen because it is easier to confine the matte effect to the proper elements when ultraviolet light is used. Ultraviolet light falling on the models gives them a slight bluish glow that has no effect if the matte is made from the orange elements of the   frame. When a blue screen is used, the light illuminating the screen is blue, and then it is very important that no blue light hit the model itself, a difficult task.

Not having to spend extra time worrying about what the light illuminates during the matte pass by using an orange screen is one of the many time and money saving techniques Legato employs to give his effects the high production values they have developed a reputation for.

"One of the things that allows you to get more money on the screen is something as stupid as matting," Legato says. "If it takes three extra hours per shot to do it, you can't get as many shots done, so you just live with fewer shots in the show. By finding a better, faster way you're able to get more shots in the same period of time, more difficult shots that appear on the screen. We learn constantly from little things like that, shooting the ships and trying to find out what would be a faster way of doing this, what would save money. Just from shooting it every day you come up with another way of doing it that's more efficient. By saving money you don't really physically save it and put it in the bank, but you now have more money for production value on the show. You don't necessarily decrease the budget, but you increase what you get from it."

The six foot model of Deep Space Nine is only one of four miniatures that collectively make up the show's permanent complement of models. The other three models are used for shots that depict the Runabout, the show's new starship/shuttle hybrid, departing from, or landing on, one of the space station's main landing pads. There is a second six foot partial model of the station that is identical to the first model except for the fact that one of the armatures is missing along with a large section of the station's core. The chunk of the station was carved away to allow the motion control camera to get up close to the station's landing pad, a shot that the jutting armatures make impossible to achieve with the complete station model.

The other two miniatures that complete the DEEP SPACE NINE set are large versions of the Runabout and a landing pad, both of which were built in scale with each other but in a much larger scale than the two models of the station itself. It was necessary to build these two models out of scale, because a Runabout model built in scale to the station   model would have been far too small to work with. Instead, the large- scale Runabout is shot arriving or departing from the large-scale landing pad, the model of the space station is shot separately, and then both shots are composited together, giving the illusion that the landing pad is part of the station.

In order to be able to shoot shots of different scale miniatures that could be successfully composited and tied together, the motion control rig built for DEEP SPACE NINE had to be of a special nodal point design. When a normal movie camera mounted on a normal camera head is panned or tilted, the camera pivots around a point below the lens and to the rear of the camera, near where the camera is mounted to the head. This is fine for normal photography, and even for miniature photography in which all of the miniatures are built to the same scale. However, when models of different scales are shot with a camera mounted on a normal motion control rig of this type, when the camera pans and tilts, the perspective changes at a different rate, depending on the scale of the model, resulting in a multi-planing effect when the different shots are composited, destroying the illusion that the models actually fit together. To avoid this problem, the DEEP SPACE NINE visual effects camera is mounted on a specially designed nodal point motion control rig that pans and tilts the camera around the camera lens itself, thus maintaining the same perspective regardless of the scale of the model being filmed.

Legato utilizes a variety of techniques to create the illusion that the space station is several orders of magnitude larger than the Enterprise, despite the fact that the space station miniature is only slightly larger than the Enterprise miniature.

"We use wider lenses than we normally do," explains Legato, "because with a wide-angle lens, if you move even a foot it looks like you've moved a tremendous distance. It creates the feeling of the station being large. We also photograph it much darker than we normally do - it's essentially backlit most of the time. That creates this great sense of depth. Everything appears to be bigger because of the way it's photographed. Everything works in concert."

Another trick used by Legato to convey a sense of enormous scale stems directly from his experiences on THE NEXT GENERATION.

"There's little tiny windows on the station," he says. "The windows on the Enterprise are always a little too big. The guy who designed it thought it would be very neat to build a space ship with really large windows. The thing that worked against that was the fact that the larger the windows, the less large the model looked. It looked small because of the window size. The smaller you make the windows, it looks like what you're shooting is enormous. Knowing better from that experience, we made all the windows smaller, we made them pin-sized."

Legato relished the opportunity DEEP SPACE NINE provided to put his own distinctive visual stamp on the look of a series. On THE NEXT GENERATION he and Dan Curry had always been constrained by the need to maintain the same tone that had been set in the initial effects shots Industrial Light and Magic had done for THE NEXT GENERATION's pilot.

"Now we can make our own look the way we want it to be," Legato points out. "There is nothing to tie into. It's essentially a brand-new start. We can shoot it any way we like. We can change the tone of it. It's a little different from what it was on THE NEXT GENERATION. We have more freedom in this thing because we're starting it ourselves. Any time you start anything new yourself you have a lot more freedom to create what it is you do, as opposed to copying what was already done."

According to Legato, the DEEP SPACE NINE look is "a little grittier than the NEXT GENERATION look. The fill level on the ships is lower, the design of the Cardassian ships is a little grimmer."

The biggest difference in Legato's approach to the visual effects is a subtle one, a difference the average viewer probably won't be able to put his or her finger on.

"The way we're programming the motion control moves is a little more live-action oriented," Legato explains. "I'm actually physically operating the camera. Whereas before we programmed each move and it was very mathematically perfect, now I program the ship move and then I follow with hand-operated wheels, just like a live-action operator would do on the stage. It has a little bit of a bump and speeds up in certain areas and slows down in others. It has a little more of a gritty, live quality to it, it's not mathematically perfect. It still looks good. You won't necessarily be able to pick it out from any one shot, but it'll give the show a distinct tone. It'll just have a different quality in the way it's photographed and the way moves are made. Ballsier would be the best way to describe it. It's darker and grittier and going for more unusual angles."

In normal motion-control photography, such as that seen on THE NEXT GENERATION, the operators program in where the camera should be on the first and last frames of a shot as well as a few select key frames during the shot, and the computer then extrapolates where the camera should be on the frames in-between the key frames. The result is an inhumanly perfect move that seems to glide through space, always keeping the ship centered on the screen no matter how torturous its path or that of the camera. The too-perfect motion controlled moves on THE NEXT GENERATION had always bothered Legato because rather than seamlessly meshing with the humanly flawed live action shots, they stood out in their perfection. If a human cameraman had actually been out in space shooting the Enterprise as it flew past, the resulting shot would have been imperfect, with some unintentional bumps and the Enterprise probably would have gone out of frame for a moment as the cameraman couldn't pan as quickly as the ship was flying past.

"When you see car pass-bys in action movies everything's not perfect," observes Legato. "It's all shaky. We're going more for that look than every frame looking absolutely perfect. That's the stylistic difference between the two shows."

Legato has encountered some difficulty in convincing some of his motion-control camera operators to follow his lead and operate some of their shots by hand.

"Some people don't like it," he admits, "because it goes against what they would normally do. If they programmed a move like that with a bump in it, they would take it out, because it's not perfect. I'm pushing this look upon the show, and I'm in a position to demand that it be shot this way. I don't think that THE NEXT GENERATION will necessarily adopt it. I don't think it'll be something that's so dramatic that people will say, 'Wow, this is really different and neat!' Basically, I'm using what amounts to old technology, STAR WARS technology. I like that look."

The same inhuman perfection that Legato finds so objectionable in purely computer-operated motion-control photography is what keeps him from embracing computer-generated visual effects, despite the fact that two frequently recurring effects in DEEP SPACE NINE, the wormhole and the transformation of Odo, the show's shape shifter, are both computer-generated.

"The reason I don't like computers that much for this particular application," explains Legato, "is that the more it looks too pristine or has a different quality to it, in and of itself it might look pretty good, but when you cut from something gritty and live-action with film grain to something absolutely clean, you are taken out of it for the moment. It looks different. It doesn't look like a camera out in space. It looks like something else. Those things are fairly subtle, but when I look at something and I say, 'I don't believe that,' then I don't believe the situation. You eliminate the suspension of disbelief in that way."

CHAPTER EIGHT
The Season Begins

David Carson, a veteran of some of THE NEXT GENERATION's most memorable episodes, including "The Enemy", "Next Phase" and "Yesterday's Enterprise", was hired to direct the pilot. As he has demonstrated, Carson has directed some of the series' most fatalistic and dark episodes.

"I have a feeling that the darker, grittier tone is one of the reasons they wanted me to direct the pilot," says Carson. "They wanted my experience with grit in STAR TREK. It is true that this will be a much grittier environment than the Enterprise, which is part of the attraction. It's my feeling that part of the grittiness of DEEP SPACE NINE is not only the setting, but the attempt to acces the slightly weaker side of human nature, while still telling extremely powerful and insightful stories."

"I don't think a good director has a style that's darker," concurs Berman. "I don't think it's darker, they're just the better directors. Paul Lynch has done some light and lovely episodes for us and so has David Carson. We basically analyzed all the directors having had the benefit of having done 126 episode of STAR TREK. David Carson is doing more, Rick Kolbe, Corey Allen, Lynch, Livingston and Les Landau are going to be directing, and those are the key guys who are going to be doing the first dozen. Every director who has done STAR TREK would like to do DEEP SPACE. We're being really picky and choosey and taking our time in deciding who's going to do it."

Despite criticism of NEXT GENERATION's idea of alien cultures being represented by people with funny forheads and crinkly noses, Rick Beman is adamant about preserving the integrity of his perception of what Roddenberry's 24th century should be. While it occassionally upsets members of his staff who want to experiment with bolder ideas, they respect his vision.

"STAR TREK, by defintion, is hokey," says Berman. "We have costumes which are obviously science-fiction costumes and make-up, but it's very important to me that make-up and prosthetics don't look like masks from a really classy Halloween store. I don't want creatures to look like monsters. I don't want people dressed like 1950's sci-fi spacemen. People flying around in space suits and in starships going at speeds faster than light and speaking perfect English and nicely breathing the same air and walking around with the same gravity is perpostrous, but it's a world we've all come to accept and use for a variety of metaphorical and entertaining reasons. Because the premise is somewhat outlandish, it is essential that the specific elements within it have to be grounded in very believable reality.

"Our characters have to deal with each other in a very believable and realistic way. The hokiest elements for me are almost more so in story and script than anywhere else. The one major input I put into the scripts tends to be after they have been beat out and written and have to deal with dialogue and plot points. They deal with keeping the dialogue believable, logical, not melodramatic, not contrived and keeping the stories clear. And keeping it from being swords and sorcery--which is a word Gene loved to use--and stay away from hokey and corny melodrama."

Following the DEEP SPACE NINE premiere, the first year will be comprised of eighteen one hour episodes and shooting will continue through May.

Once the pilot script was completed, Piller along with his team of writer/producers Ira Steven Behr and Peter Allan Fields, who trade-off rewrites of material purchased from freelancers, turned their attention to the upcoming season.

"I think you can always take chances in the first season on a show like this," says Ira Steven Behr. "We haven't become fossilized. It's not like you're going to have six episodes and get cancelled. You have chances to do things first year and chances in the fifth and sixth season, where you've done everything and you can say make it a western or put them all naked in the holodeck. Those are the times to really have fun. The second and the third season when suddenly you've made it, things tend to get a little bit stodgier on most television shows. This is a fun time to be here -- hopefully."

The writers have also made themselves accessible to the cast who are still in the process of defining the characters.

"Occasionally I'll ring too see if he's too spacey or if he's a wimp or something and they'll say 'No, just carry on'," explains El Faddil. "The writers are just making it up as they go along and I'm just going along with that. I quite enjoy the luxury of watching where it develops and seeing where it goes. It's the third project I've ever done in my life and it's interesting. Of course, in a few months, I'll probably say 'Yes, I want to fight someone or be an alien for a day.'"

Rene Auberjonois, says he rarely talks to the producers unless it's necessary, unlike his previous experience on television.

"If I come upon something, a word or two in a script I may speak with them," says the actor. "I spent six years doing BENSON and it's a very different process where you sit at the table with the writers and you talk through the script. That does not happen here. They're much more complicated and they have to be structured and built more carefully. I'm just so happy with the character and the stories that we've had to do."

"I've made calls when I've read a script and something's cut out," says actress Nana Visitor of her relationship with the producers. "It doesn't happen very often, usually the scripts stay pretty much the same, but I've called Rick and we've had discussions and asked him why and talked about how I feel. It's productive and he's been very available in that sense. It's not like 'Oh god, here are the producers.'"

"As with everything in television, it's gearing your mind in a certain direction," says Ira Behr of writing for DEEP SPACE. "Writing is discipline, that's what everybody says. The difference between people who can write and people who can't, besides talent, comes down to discipline, which evokes a lot of other things as well. You have to realize the parameters of what you're doing. We sit around and come up with great thoughts and possibilities that cannot and will not be done. We have a good budget for this show, the highest budget on television. Nontheless, we still don't do action all that well or a lot. We have some space battles, but the most action I've ever seen on this show was BEST OF BOTH WORLDS, which had shooting and running down corridors. So you're forced to do more cerebral and thoughtful and less intense television, which I guess kind of fits into the Gene Roddenberry world which isn't people slapping each other in the face and drive-by shootings in space."

During the production meetings, Behr explains, is when the impact of production realities can best be felt limiting his ability as a writer to visualize the story he hopes to put on screen.

"You get cranky over the course of a season," says Behr. "Everything will kind of wear you down a bit and we'll have those wonderful production meetings and hear those dreaded words, you haven't met pattern and this show is above pattern and you've got to get rid of a scene. The guest cast on DEEP SPACE is going to be a lot different than that of THE NEXT GENERATION, we're going to have more people. It's a space station. There will be more speaking roles to show more people inahbit this environment. Unfortunatley, the more speaking roles you have, the higher the budget is for guest cast and you've got to make it up someplace else--the sets or opticals, and stuff like that. As I wrote my first script, one of the things I thought as I was going over it, was dare he speak? Dare they speak? Well, dare I take out this optical so this person might be able to speak? It sounds fun and sometimes it *is* fun and it's creative, but by the 12th show it's like how many more weeks till the end of the season? It doesn't matter how you feel about the show and it's not about whether you love or hate your job. It's just survival."

Behr notes with some irony that while the original STAR TREK is prided for its allegorical exploration of then-contemporary socio-political concerns, the perception of the show has been altered by the passing of time. The same, he feels, will happen with DEEP SPACE NINE.

"I like the shows," says Behr. "I like to be proud of the shows. What I find with the old series is what you think you're saying, 20 years later turns out not to be what you were saying at all. The potlitical winds change and since we have to deal with things on such a fundamental, banal level, even when it comes to the quality shows, it's not really examining the human condition in a really deep way. I think none of us know until they tell us what we did 50 years from now. We're trying to do an hour of television a week that we can be proud of and is entertaining and that can be thoughtful in some ways and, ultimately, leave enough behind us that could be sold at conventions. People will want to take the memos and the handwritten little notes we've sent each other and study them for hours and figure out what we meant. And if they find out what we meant, they should call me and tell me because half the time I don't know what I mean."

"There's always another level to it," says actor Rene Auberjonois. "We did an episode which is a classic STAR TREK script in that it's full of pyrotechnics and special effects and incredible stunts, but beyond that it deals with something. It's about a man being hunted who's not a man, he's a creature. On the surface it's about a fox hunt. It's in the future and it's about an alien race chasing this creature through space and how it impacts on our lives and our world. I shot an episode about Odo called 'A Man Alone', which really deals with prejudice where people turn on him as a freak and suspect him of something he's innocent of. You could say on one level it's just a murder mystery, but on another level it goes beyond that. The show consistently does that and I'm real happy about it. It's nice to earn a living and not be embarassed by what you're doing."

"That's one fo the reasons for its longeviity," echoes Siddig El Faddil. "But also it's important that its not pretentious. The stable of writers they've gotten try and get something underneath, but how many people actually connect DEEP SPACE NINE with the problems of Eastern Europe at the moment? The writers try to do that and sometimes it's not that subtle. For instance, there's a whole episode about how to deal with death or children or education. They're worthy scripts, but it's dangerous to get pretentious about it."

Ask anyone ever involved with STAR TREK: THE NEXT GENERATION and they'll tell you the hardest part of making the series has been finding writers who can craft stories that work within the paramaters of the universe established by Gene Roddenberry. DEEP SPACE NINE takes place in the same universe but, thanks to the inclusion of non-Starfleet personnel as regulars, there's more leeway for conflict between the characters. As anyone on either show would attest, it's a godsend for those creating their adventures.

"We're always desperately looking for writers," says Executive Producer Rick Berman. "We lost [TNG Story Editor] Joe Menosky because he decided to take a respite, but we have two television shows and we have a wonderful group of people writing NEXT GENERATION--Jeri Taylor and Brannon Braga and Rene Echevaria--and we're very pleased. In terms of DEEP SPACE NINE, we went back in to get Ira Behr and Peter Fields over from NEXT GENERATION, and it came down to who was going to make up the remainder of our writing staff. In terms of both shows the rule we have is we don't hire anybody, no matter who they are and what kind of reputation they have, unless they have written an episode sucessfully for us."

That particular rule grew out of the fact that many competent writers had been brought aboard THE NEXT GENERATION before cutting their teeth on a 24th century tale, often resulting in a short-lived tenure and an early departure. Apparently, equally important is using your middle name.

"I've done television for 11 years and there is no show more difficult that I've ever been involved with than STAR TREK on a number of levels," says Ira Steven Behr. "It's just difficult because you're not just trying to tell a story that could work or not work, you're trying to tell a story that works within very special, limited parameters. The only thing I can compare an episode of STAR TREK to is another episode of STAR TREK. The rules are so clear and it's such a unique kind of thing that in the third season of THE NEXT GENERATION I would come up with ideas that I would think would be really good and work that other people would say you can't do. And I'd go we can't do this, we can't do that but we should do this and now it's maybe not. All I know is now when I think of things, I think how does it fit into the 30 years of STAR TREK that came before it? I think that helps me from falling into the really, really big traps that it's easy to fall into that you're going to reinvent the show. Every writer who's ever had an axe to grind, and there are definitely axes to grind, has complained about that. Having been through that fire, that ordeal, I'm not quite at that same place. I'm not saying we need more violence or we need more action or whatever it is, or we need to tackle something really, really controversial, because on the other side lies madness. The other way to go is, ultimately, you leave because it's just too difficult. DEEP SPACE NINE at this point is about as open as you're going to get. We'll see what happens at the end of the year and we'll look at it and see what we have."

"Everything is so settled on THE NEXT GENERATION since all the conflict must come from external sources," agrees DEEP SPACE Producer and Story Editor Peter Allan Fields. "In DEEP SPACE NINE, these people don't know each other that well. Some are Starfleet, some are Federation and the majority on the station is not. It's the CASABLANCA analogy, a place with strangers coming in and out and all sorts of things going on. Our people are getting to know each other as well as the station and anything that can go wrong will go wrong. If you think that makes it easier to write, it doesn't. It promises to be as much fun as THE NEXT GENERATION, but on the other hand there ain't nothing wrong with the NEXT GENERATION either."

Fields joined the STAR TREK writing staff fifth season after having contributed year four's euthanasia allegory, "Half a Life." A veteran of such series' as HELLINGER'S LAW (with Michael Piller), THE MAN FROM U.N.C.L.E. and THE SIX MILLION DOLLAR MAN, he joined the writing staff of DEEP SPACE NINE following the completion of TREK's fifth season. Also recruited onboard the writing staff of DEEP SPACE NINE was writer/producer Behr, who since having left the show at the end of its third season, contributed the fourth season STAR TREK episode "Q-pid" and sold a big-budget period action film to Joel Silver, HICOCK & CODY, which has Harrison Ford attached to star. Behr had first been approached by Maurice Hurley second season when he was working at Paramount on the NBC series THE BRONX ZOO, but rebuffed overtures to join the series when he went out to lunch with the former TREK producer.

"He told me what it would entail to work on the show and I said 'Goodbye, thank you'," says Behr. "It was just very different than I was used to on series television."

Before discovering the STAR TREK universe, Behr had worked on the short-lived ABC series ONCE A HERO, and the MGM syndicated series FAME, which was, ironically, one of his first encounters with televised science-fiction.

"I did three years on FAME which was a lot of fun and was also in syndication. We had no one looking over our shoulder," says Behr. "We got to do some wonderfully bizarre things on the show and the only time they gave us any trouble was the last show I was going to write after I knew we were cancelled. It was going to be ROAD WARRIOR meets FAME. It was a show that takes place in the future and you could only sing for the state. It was a fascist society and we were going to have motorcycles going through the school and have Iggy Pop as the guest star. It was great and I was in the midst of writing the episode when somehow MGM read somewhere that we planned to burn down the set, which was a lie. We were going to trash them a bit, but it wasn't the last episode. We had one more after that and they stopped me from writing it. We had a lot of fun doing that show."

Behr was eventually persuaded by Michael Piller to join the writing staff during the series' still tumultuous third season. He left at the end of his first year after penning "Captain's Holiday" and "The Vengeance Factor" and contributing to numerous other rewrites.

"When I had left NEXT GENERATION they offered me a two year deal for the fourth and fifth season which, after going back and forth on, I decided not to take," recalls Behr. "I spent the last two years in feature development. I had three films in development including one at Warner Bros but Michael [Piller] always kept the door open for me and we'd go to a ball game every year or something like that. I got a call from Michael about doing 'Q-pid' and he wanted to know if I wanted to do it. I came in, we met, went off, wrote it, stopped by one day to watch them film. It was written and filmed while I was waiting to do a rewrite on HICOCK & CODY. The whole process was begun and done while I'm waiting for notes, so it shows you the difference between the two mediums. The writing is fun. I would tell anyone that writing a feature is a helluva lot more fun that writing television. It's just much fuller and richer in certain ways, but except for the writing. Television is a lot more fun as a whole because you're with people. You're breaking stories in a room, you're watchng dailies every day, the set is there."

Shortly thereafter, Piller once again approached Behr about being involved with a spin-off series.

"Michael had talked to me a long time ago about doing a sequel or a spin-off to STAR TREK," says Behr. "He said, 'I don't know where you're going to be but we'd love to get you involved with it.' I said, 'I'll think about it.' I found it interesting and they kept talking about stuff like darker and grittier and more character conflict and I said, 'Okay' and he said 'We're going to do this thing, do you want to get into it?'"

Ultimately, Behr admits that the final decision about whether to come onboard involved monetary considerations, an important arbiter for any full-time writer.

"I met with Rick and Michael and basically, though this does not sound like something people would be interested to read, it basically came down to money, career," says Behr. "I have three movies in feature development but it just doesn't pay the money that I could get doing this. It was partially financial and it partially gave me a chance to step back and let these things happen and get in on the ground floor of something that's going to take on a life of its own and be very huge. There's something fun about that."

Already Behr has found life in the 24th century a far cry from his previous duty aboard the Enterprise.

"I think one of the things I'm enjoying so far about being on the show is the working relationship I have with Peter Allan Fields," says Behr. "He's a hoot. The guy's got stories from the MAN FROM U.N.C.L.E. on, and he's one of the brightest guys in the business. And he's as strange a character as I am. I think one day we should do a twosome on the road to the conventions. I never thought about going to a convention in my life, but if I could introduce Peter to the STAR TREK people I would do that. It's like he's the last of his tribe, the old pro from Dover."

Fields echoes Behr's enthusiasm for working on DEEP SPACE NINE while admitting it hasn't been easy work with Behr, Piller and himself alternating rewrites while remaining true to the Roddenberry ethos.

"Hard work can be fun," says Fields. "We have concerns about whether we're doing things right and I don't know what that is. I think we're being true to what Gene Roddenberry has envisioned and I perosnally have come to this belatedly. I've gotten a far better view than I ever thought I would have. He meant what he espoused and the work comes from keeping within his parameters. I can't give you some great profound statement, but I *can* tell you there's a standard which this show certainly complements, which I personally take pleasure in helping to promologate. It's not just that audiences remember what went before and so you better do such and such now because otherwise you're going to get nasty letters. That's probably true, but it's more in keeping faith in what we're doing. Of all the shows I've worked on over many years, this is the hardest and also the most rewarding. I've never had this experience and I would not have missed it for anything."

While Behr acknowledges that five years of doing STAR TREK has helped the writers avoid a plethora of traps, there are roads not taken that DEEP SPACE NINE will need to explore on its own--without having learned the lessons taught by previous TREKS.

"Rick will say a million times the experience of doing THE NEXT GENERTION is obviously coming in handy," says Behr. "We're in a better position than we were with 'Farpoint' which was from scratch. But at the same time, it's a television show and the farther we get away from TNG the more we will fall into our own traps and see things that don't quite work. We'll make mistakes and it sort of gives you an opportunity to make a choice, bad and good, and we'll make them both. The thing I learned is it doesn't matter if it's good or bad, it's whether its good or bad in STAR TREK terminology."

The biggest lesson the creators of the new show learned was the need for conflict between the characters, and that can be found in abundance on DEEP SPACE.

Behr hypothesizes that a lot of the depth may be lost on some viewers who will resort to traditional anaylsis without looking at the deeper subtexts and drama inherent in the show.

"I think the arguments are still going to be based on who do you like better," sighs Behr. "Picard or Kirk or Sisko? What do you think? Does that set look better than Ten Forward? Odo or Data? Dax or Spock? That's the level of this. It's not fundamentally that much different. It's just different enough to exist as itself."

Like many of the writers who have toiled on the final frontier, Behr is not a big fan of STAR TREK.

"The thing that I find about NEXT GENERATION is that they all really love STAR TREK," says Behr. "I think that gives a core of solidarity that kind of helps the show because it's one of those shows that really works best when people give a damn about the whole mythos of STAR TREK. I watched the first three seasons of STAR TREK when it came out back in the 60's and I was a fan. My older sister and I watched it every week, but when the show went off the air I never was a Trekkie, never cared much about it. I enjoyed the series when it was on the air from '66-'69, but I would have been just as happy if Jeffrey Hunter had played the lead. I liked him a lot too. I never watched NEXT GENERATION except once or twice before I came on staff."

Not surprisingly, Behr would be happy to avoid any further cross-overs between DEEP SPACE NINE and the show's orginal cast of characters, as has been done several times in THE NEXT GENERATION.

"I would rather bring the kids from FAME back than the old STAR TREK characters because that bridge has been crossed," says Behr. "It's now who do you bring back? Is it Sulu? Is it Chekov? Do we bring back James Doohan again? I liked McCoy growing up the most. He was the character I most liked as a kid and he was brought back already -- and that was the character that I would have had the most fun with. And they put him, of all people, in the 137 year old make-up. At least Scotty came back and had a shot at being Scotty."

Early on during the series' development it had been difficult to generate story ideas since outside writers hadn't been exposed to the series yet. As Behr tells it, they certainly tried anyway.

"It's not like the NEXT GENERATION people even waited to see the show," says Behr. "I would like to take everyone out who has tried to write a story, written a story, got hired to write a story and got cut-off on a story and buy them dinner. It's like into the valley of death road the 600. These people took a wing and a prayer, some of them went off before we cast the show, while the sets were being built, and all they had to read was this pilot with all these new characters and a new environment that none of them knew. It's tough to hit a home-run under those circumstances as a writer. I would not like to have done it. So it all winds up falling on our shoulders and, basically, Michael is running back and forth between both shows. Day to day it's Pete and myself and we love each other dearly, but we would love to add more people on staff because they want someone to write a show and prove themselves. I'm hopeful, but doubtful, I'll be able to write a show this season of my own. It'll probably be rewrite city for the rest of the season. Maybe when we start to hit shows 17 and 18 we can start to do them from scratch. It's much more fun sometimes to be the audience and I like the times when I can be an audience as well as a member of the creative team behind the show, because it's just a lot more fun to say, 'That thing sucks, I could do better than that' or 'That's really great man, those guys must be geniuses.'"

For Behr, the adulation that has endeared TREK to millions of fanatical followers is difficult to fathom. Almost as difficult as those who would label those who labor on the staffs of television shows creating entertainment the cultural elite.

"If the people who do television are the cultural elite then this country doesn't deserve to survive," says Behr. "And it probably won't ultimately, because this country is a country that has no concept of culture at all. From it's very foundation this country has always been suspicious of its artists and there has always been that Puritan strain that began this country. I think we all have fears that no matter what we do, STAR TREK will overshadow it. It's something best not to dwell on, which is why I feel the level of it is too bizarre. There's a lot of good things out there in the creative arts, great books that have been written. Superb books, interesting movies, interesting plays. People should be sitting around talking about THE SOUND AND THE FURY, and people going to conventions to try and figure out how someone can write that book or WAITING FOR GODOT. That to me is popular entertainment, as popular as anything that deserves a level of recognition. This gets that kind of recognition because, basically, life is full of jokes and we don't know and don't understand what goes on. It's a nice thing when you meet someone who you're never going to see again and you say 'I work on STAR TREK, goodbye,' and they leave going, 'Oh, that's wonderful' -- but you don't want to see those people again."

Behr is wary of those who would read too much signifcance into the meaning of the show, pointing out that even the series' postulated utopian ethos are inherently distopian.

"To get there you have to believe in a utopian view and I believe in a more distopian view only because I know what I believe in is what I see," says Behr. "I think DEEP SPACE NINE is an optimistic show and is predicated on the thought that human beings are basically going to rise above the situation we currently find ourselves in. The flaw in the thinking is it doesn't explain how we ever got there and that's too big an issue to ever discuss. Whenever McFarland, who does all those weird movie and television books, does a book about what STAR TREK actually means and the deep philosophy of STAR TREK, they'll figure out whether we were ultimately a utopian or distopian show."

As the writers continue to ply their trade, they discover more about the world of DEEP SPACE NINE. And even as viewers become more familar with the new TREK universe, the writers continue to learn more about their creation as well.

"That's the adventure of this series," says Peter Fields. "I'm not coming into something that's already established as is NEXT GENERATION. When I switched over to DEEP SPACE NINE it was at the countdown and it was an adventurous ride that's now taking off. I'm very glad to be writing it. I don't know the destination but the ride, so far, with Mike and Ira is great."

Behr agrees that like THE NEXT GENERATION, which many feel didn't come into its own until its third season, DEEP SPACE will wobble a little before finding its space legs. During the summer hiatus, the writers can assess their first year and approach the show's sophmore year a little wiser.

"I think that we will learn, just like the audience will learn and the show will take on a life of it's own. We'll have a better feel for the show after finishing the first year, but there is something nice about flying by the seat of your pants that first season. It's fun because so many times we sit there and think things that we thought would suck turn out to be great, and things we thought were gong to play like gangbusters don't. The actor or the director may not take it the way we foresaw. Second season, hopefully, those questions have been answered to a certain extent. Then you can sit like a pompous ass behind your desk and make pronouncements to people.

"This year the freelancers come in shaking," laughs Behr. "They're looking for direction and we look at them and say 'We don't know, you tell us. I'm not sure' and they go back and they say 'Fucked again.' That's why they hate being freelancers. In the second season you say 'Do this and if you don't, you're out'."

One of the most exciting developments for the writers has been exploring the life of the station. Unlike, the Enterprise which is boldly going, examing the space station requires looking inwards as opposed to outwards.

"Kira and Sisko I think have an interesting relationship and Dax and Sisko and Dax and Bashir," says Behr. "They all link in strange and unusual ways and I think that's a lot of fun. Because it is a space station and we're basically there and people come to us, we have to keep showing the life of this place. Unlike the Enterprise, in which the excitement obviously happens on the bridge or in Ten Forward or the Captain's Ready Room. Here it's not that clear, so we're forced by circumstance to find more places and more people. I'm hoping guest cast will start becoming semi-regulars. We had a wonderful performance by Andrew Robinson [DIRTY HARRY, HELLRAISER] who played Garrick and he's terrific. He played this Cardassian left on the station, the only one, who runs a clothing shop and he's a spy. Everyone kind of knows he's a spy, but he'll never admit he's a spy, and he's trying to get Bashir as kind of an ally. It was just a wonderful thing. I'm not saying Garrick is going to come back, but just the thought that he *might*. He's a good enough character that he could."

Costume designer Bob Blackman stocked Garrick's tailor shop with a virtual stockpile of previous TREK ware.

"It's a pretty amazing tailor shop where we pulled a lot of our old stuff together," he says. "It's kind of a history of what I've done on STAR TREK hanging on the racks. We're now beginning to do ship shows on NEXT GENERATION where they don't go off the ship and we're also doing space station shows. The problem is that they haven't evolved all the areas of the space station, so everytime they come to a new one it's always interesting."

CHAPTER NINE
Treks into Deep Space

One advantage that DEEP SPACE NINE has had since it began shooting is both narrative and logistical synergy with its sister series, STAR TREK: THE NEXT GENERATION. Using the wealth of material created over six years on STAR TREK, Piller and his writing staff have injected the series with friendly reminders that they're in a familar territory.

"The creative synergy allows you incredible opportunities," says Piller. "We've used Picard in the pilot, we've used Lursa and Bator in show two and we've used Q and Vash in the context of guest starring roles. What I'm most delighted about is that we're not leaning on them."

For those who missed Q last year on the final frontier, he'll be making up for it sixth season with two appearances on both STAR TREK: THE NEXT GENERATION as well as on DEEP SPACE NINE, where Benjamin Sisko and his crew of Starfleet officers will have their own chance to grapple with the omnipotent super-being. After all, why should Picard have all the fun?

"Vash and Q come back," says writer/producer Ira Steven Behr. "A writer came in with a story that now bears little resemblance to what's going to end up. She had an archeologist involved with something weird and from that we said if it's a beautiful archeologist, we can make that Vash. We started to try and make that show work and Michael and I were talking and I said, 'It probably would be helpful if we could bring Q in', and he said 'Yeah, bring in Q. Let's do it.' We're open for that kind of stuff.

"At the beginning when we talked about doing this sort of stuff, we'd go slinking off saying that's a crutch, is that going to be a good idea right off the bat to be thinking in those terms like what can we do with Mrs. Troi or Lore, Data's brother? But after watching the early shows you realize this show is so different than NEXT GENERATION in terms of its feel, that we're not worried about that. We could even bring Picard back if we wanted, not that that's anything we're thinking about, but it still wouldn't be in danger of looking too much like what's come before. It's a different show."

Continues Behr about his use of Q and Vash, a character he created for NEXT GENERATION's "Captain's Holiday" and one of Picard's first sexual dalliances on the series, "One of the things I think people feel about some of these characters is that whether you like them or not, and I know plenty of people who I have to explain that it wasn't my idea to do Robin Hood, look at me like you're some kind of a fucking hack doing this stupid STAR TREK show. But there are others who say they're the fun and humorous episodes, the characters have a lot of life to them and they're fun shows."

Lursa and Bator, the treacherous Klingon plotters of STAR TREK's "Redemption", return for considerably more sinister purposes than showing off their ample cleavage in Bob Blackman's revealing female Klingon costumes.

"The creative synergy allows you incredible opportunities," says Piller. "It's interesting how we've used them. Essentially, we have a story and, in the case of Lursa and Bator, we said 'Hey we've got a real kind of CASABLANCA spy story and we need someone to really be doing double dealings and bringing money and doing gun exchanges. Why don't we use the Klingons and use those characters that we love so much?' It works out just fine to use those guys because then there's a connection and an identification.There's a backstory, there's a history and all of these things make for a much richer series."

Says Ira Behr, "There's no doubt that people like Lwaxana's [Troi], and Q and Vash and a bunch of others have a certain life to them as characters and an energy that certainly helps the NEXT GENERATION and could help us too. The characters that don't have to be Starfleet and don't have those strings we have attached so often. A lot of times you have people performing those characters who take a lot of relish in doing them, so they're fun to have come back."

Piller doesn't feel that by exploiting NEXT GENERATION's voluminous history, DEEP SPACE NINE will be at an unfair advantage appealing only to those familar with STAR TREK lore.

"You have to look at the shows themselves," says Piller. "There's no question in my mind that, conceptually, each of these shows would work because they're about the new characters. In the episode with Lursa and Bator, there's a moral dilemma for Major Kira where she has to confront her loyalty to her past life and what her new life is going to be. It's really about her. It's illuminating our new characters. As I've always said on both shows, the guest stars are the cataylsts. There have been times when I have not been satisfied, more prior to my arrival, that the shows have been about the guest stars, but ultimately the shows that succeed are when the guest stars are serving as catalysts to illuminate our characters."

Equally advantageous has been the production synergy which has allowed both series to utilize sets and props from the other. The addition of three soundstages of 24th century sets has proved an asset to NEXT GENERATION's production. The man responsible for overseeing production over the entire TREK universe is David Livingston.

"I am the one person who knows what's going on both shows from a production end," says Livingston. "One of my jobs has been to cross-pollinate. On NEXT GENERATION we required a seedy kind of bar which a Ferengi was hanging out in. We used one of the sets on DEEP SPACE NINE to do it with a minimal amount of redressing so we saved a substantial amount of money. Using elements from both shows we're able to deliver more to the audience for less cost. Normally, in the past, you would have had to cut a scene. For instance, the Ferengi scene was going to be cut until we thought about how could we do it cheaper and one of the ways was to use one of the existing sets on DEEP SPACE NINE. So instead of that scene being cut from the picture, we were able to find something that was already existing on another show. In another episode we use the alien shuttle from NEXT GENERATION, which Herman used to good effect. Michael Westmore is using aliens on both shows. We're trying to make sure the episodes don't air real close to each other, but he'll create an alien for one show and we'll use it on the other. Bob Blackman is doing the same thing with costumes. We're trying to reuse and recycle, but not so the audience will ever know."

As costume designer for both, Blackman has also helped oversee the natural synergy between the two shows that has allowed him to maximize his production dollars in creating wardrobe.

"My favorite thing is we did 12 Cardassian suits for the pilot and then we got to use 11 of them on NEXT GENERATION," says Blackman. "They just wrote the Cardassians right in. I love that there's already that crossover between the two shows because they kept the time-frame the same and one's not a prequel or a sequel. We have this great opportunity to mix and match and we do."

An area in which the synergistic relationship has proven particularly helpful has been in dressing the myriad aliens which inhabit DEEP SPACE NINE.

"There are aliens walking around on the Promenade that you have seen in the NEXT GENERATION, so we give the notion that the universe is travelling, that this is just kind of this floating hotel, this United Nations idea of a place in space," says Blackman. "I find it wonderful. We're creating every week for DEEP SPACE NINE whereas on NEXT GENERATION it is primarily humanoid with a small smattering of aliens. It is the converse on this show with a small smattering of humans constantly facing one kind of alien after another. I used to refer to it as alien of the week like movies of the week and now disease of the week telefilms, but now it's aliens of the week. We recycle some, we mix components that we have in stock."

Another frequent collaborator with Blackman is veteran Make-Up Supervisor Michael Westmore, who is responsible for creating the aliens Blackman has to dress.

"It's a little harder this year because the both of us are trying to figure out how we get these two big machines to work and not end up in little padded cells or satin lined boxes at the end of April," laughs Blackman of his peer who also shares responsibilities for overseeing both TREK shows. "We don't have quite as much collaboration as we did but we do talk on the phone. For instance, when we did our first Cardassian civilian I had to do a nine year old girl--which is just great--to try and figure out what to do with these civilians in what has been defined as a military community. How much of those certain design factors do you employ so you get the image? It's obviously television and it's kind of visual bites. I try to keep things in a simplistic form; all Klingons have certain things that go on their uniforms and all Romulans have shoulders and Cardassians have this funny taper. Certainly these are things when you see them you can immediately identify, just as in sports you can tell what sport it is. If it's football, you can tell by the shoulder pads, it doesn't matter what color the uniform is. As in baseball, it's the same idea and then you break it up into teams."

"The two staffs are necessarily, completely autonomous," adds Herman Zimmerman, who notes that there is little personnel crossover between the two sister series. "We have much too much work to do. Where it's possible, we'll certainly cooperate. We've used alot of props from NEXT GENERATION because, frankly, we haven't had the time to generate all the props that we need for the stories here. We borrowed furniture from Jimmy Meese and setpieces from Richard James and vice versa. They've found a couple of ocassions this season to use our sets and borrow some of our artifacts, which is as it should be. We did have the Enterprise on the pilot and used several of the sets from NEXT GENERATION. But in series, we probably won't see the Enterprise very often. There's certainly cross polinazation possible and in stories in NEXT GENERATION we may see some of our characters over there. But the thrust of the series is to have it stand on its own."

Ankling STAR TREK to take over as Director of Photography of DEEP SPACE NINE was three year TREK veteran, Marvin Rush. Taking over behind the camera of NEXT GENERATION is Jonathan West, who was discovered by David Livingston.

"I was given his reel and I took one look at it and I said this is him," notes Livingston. "It didn't matter about meeting him, finding out his background, how much money he wanted, who his crew was. None of that mattered because we knew this was the guy for us. Fortunately everything else fell into place perfectly. It was a seamless transition and we're thrilled to have him. The shows are indicative of what a good director of photography he is, and to have a camerman like that who wants to do episodic television is wonderful. I said, 'Why would you want to come in and do a show where the look is a set?' and he said, 'Because I know that you allow the DP to do his or her job.' He had heard about Planet Hell, where we have the swing sets and where the DP is allowed to do stuff and to create a look and we don't dictate it to him. That in general is what NEXT GENERATION and, hopefully, DEEP SPACE NINE is about. We allow the creative people to do their job and that's what intrigued him about coming to do our show, because he was going to be able to do unusual and different things. The remark I use is if you can't do it on STAR TREK, where can you do it? It's the same way with directors.

They like to do our show because we allow them to direct, we're not like other shows in tow where someone stands on stage looking over their shoulder. We pay the directors alot of money and you have to use them if you're going to hire them."

The key to success, according to Livingston, has been a management style that has encouraged creative freedom and pride in the state-of-the art craftsmanship that goes into producing an episode of STAR TREK.

"It's good people," says Livingston. "The mark of good management is to hire the best people you can get and let them do the work. Fortunately we've been able to find the kind of people who are interested in this kind of material and who are really good at what they do. DEEP SPACE NINE brought over a lot of people from the NEXT GENERATION and some are doing double duty. Mike Okuda, Rick Sternbach, Michael Westmore and Bob Blackman are pulling double duty."

Michael Piller enthuses about the sixth year stories of STAR TREK: THE NEXT GENERATION, which he feels has improved over the previous year's offerings. He is still responsible for working with Jeri Taylor in developing material.

"I'm happier with the story generation on THE NEXT GENERATION than I've been in a long time," says Piller. "I think we have better stories this season than we did last season, and it hasn't really started this season. It started the end of last season. Rick and I both said let's have more fun with this. Let's open it up and let your imagination run a little wild, and the response has been terrific. We've really done a lot of colorful shows. There will be some who say it's old STAR TREK and it's hokey, but I think it's a wonderfully entertaining and imaginative show. My role has only been as the guide to make sure we don't go too far, the mix is still comfortable, that we're not forgetting what has been very successful for us in terms of character development and truly exploring the human condition, and doing shows of social importance. The execution of that has been almost entirely the responsibility of Jeri Taylor. I've done very little writing on the NEXT GENERATION. I read scripts, stories, notes, and I look at structures, but she has put together a working operation with Ron Moore, Brannon Braga and Rene Echevaria."

Rick Berman is quick to refute charges from fans that with all the effort being directed towards DEEP SPACE NINE, NEXT GENERATION is being allowed to wither. In contrast, he feels sixth season has been one of the show's strongest yet.

"I think we're just having alot more fun this year on the series," says Berman of NEXT GENERATION. "We did an episode where we took all our regulars and turned them into kids and cowboys, and we brought Scotty back and I think there has been some very imaginative stories. We've allowed a little more fun to come into it. We also felt there wasn't enough science-fiction last season and we've tried to inject some of that back."

Berman has few doubts that DEEP SPACE NINE will ultimately meet with the success that both of its progenitors have had over the years.

"And in '95 I'll have a third or a fourth series," laughs Berman, saying he could have never predicted the unprecedented success of NEXT GENERATION and his role in creating the spin-off space opera. "Leaving a well paying job at a movie studio in 1987 to go to work on a science-fiction sequel syndicated television series was a big risk for me. I had a lot of people who told me I was nuts, but I had a feeling it was going to work and I decided it was worth the risk. I am now obviously very confident DEEP SPACE NINE will be equally as successful."

With NEXT GENERATION and DEEP SPACE NINE running concurrently, Berman harbors hopes that the two series will be sufficently unique to keep viewers interested in both universes.

"It'll be a little different than NEXT GENERATION, but keep the flavor of STAR TREK and Roddenberry's future and at the same time have fun and develop the characters," predicts Berman of DEEP SPACE's first year on the air. "We're starting to do that already and keep it fun. The only way you can do what I do and what Mike does is to take this stuff very seriously. You have to stay very devoted to it and put in a tremendous amount of dedication. It's hard to do that if you're not having some degree of fun. I think the key is to keep it fun and keep the actors and the directors and everyone who is making the show comfortable with one another and feeling pride in what they're doing. I just want to keep doing that."

"I can always say that I was there on the first day of shooting of DEEP SPACE NINE," says Ira Behr. "We all went down to the set, which is something we don't do alot on this show, as opposed to a lot of other television shows. We wanted to be there at the beginning so we could all say we were on the set looking at day one. I have very little emotional sentimentality about this series, but being on the set that day was definitely a kick and I'm glad I was there. It was fun and hopefully we'll have the same reaction THE NEXT GENERATION had the first year."

One of the hardest tasks Piller faced as Executive Producer of NEXT GENERATION was finding 26 producible stories a year. Fortunately for DEEP SPACE NINE's first season, the show's mid-season pick-up has allowed them the luxury of only having to produce 18 episodes following the two-hour opener.

Says Piller. "THE NEXT GENERATION is in development 52 weeks a year and that will have to be the same case with DEEP SPACE NINE. The hardest thing to come up with is ideas. We have to wait and hope somebody will walk in the door with a new idea that we'll get excited about. Fortunately, they always do."

CHAPTER TEN
Beyond Deep Space-- SF's Other Odd Numbered Space Station

Writer/producer J. Michael Straczynski, the creative force behind such shows as CAPTAIN POWER and THE NEW TWILIGHT ZONE, has finally been able to realize his dream project. Five years in the making, Straczynski and producer Doug Netter convinced Warner Bros. to back their proposed telefilm, "The Gathering", pilot for a new science-fiction series, BABYLON 5.

"I've appeared on convention panels called 'Why Can't They Do It Right?', about television science-fiction, and asked the fans what aren't you happy with?" says Straczynski. "'What do you not want to see anymore?' I couldn't tell them about BABYLON 5, but I just wanted to get a sense about what pissed them off as viewers. That's why our unofficial BABYLON 5 motto is 'No Cute Kids or Robots...Ever!' In a way, with great power comes great responsibility, as it went with Peter Parker. This is the show they've been asking for without knowing what they've been asking for."

BABYLON 5 is a three mile wide space station which boasts everything from casinos to bazaars to alien environments with different gravities and atmospheres, as well as living quarters, shops and docking bays. Most of the sets are swing sets, which means they can be redressed to be different parts of the station. One standing set is the main corridor, an elaborate 120 foot circular tube through which those on the station travel both on foot and people-movers.

"If I had one image in my head it was that of Venice in 1600 or 1700 when it was a trading port for the whole world," says costume designer Catherine Adair. "It was an open free port and I put that city into the future in my head. What would it be like? That's the one image that I said to them in my first meeting and I kept it with me. We all talked about Casablanca, Venice, Marakesh, Jerusalem--where I was--and I remember being fascinated by seeing the very, very old and the very,very new and everything in between. That's the sense I've had of BABYLON 5."

"I like to call it STAR TREK TO NOWHERE," laughs production designer John Iacovelli. "It's not about seeking out new worlds and that kind of thing, although there are new things that happen. It's more like HILL STREET BLUES or ST. ELSEWHERE in the sense that we care about these people and [explore] what makes us care about them."

Unlike the producers of most genre television shows, Straczynski, a former journalist, is a longtime science-fiction fan whose credits include story editing THE REAL GHOSTBUSTERS, JAKE & THE FATMAN and, currently, MURDER, SHE

WROTE. He's familiar with the refrain among genre aficionados that, except for TREK, television hasn't done justice to science-fiction.

One aspect that Straczynski promises will differentiate BABYLON 5 from STAR TREK or any other shows of its ilk, is the fact that the characters and the universe they inhabit are far from utopian. In fact, the world of the future is very much like the one we inhabit today except that it's populated by denizens from several alien empires and features previously unseen futuristic technology.

"In the STAR TREK universe we've overcome everything," notes Straczynski. "The policy among the writers of that series is that the characters can have no inner doubts or flaws or fears, and I think the process of overcoming is more interesting than having overcome. It is more dramatically interesting. These are characters that are trying to get along. The whole premise of BABYLON 5 is we've got Eastern Europe and East LA falling apart and we're trying to learn, as Rodney King said, to get along. The premise of BABYLON 5 is if you can get along with someone with five arms and six limbs, you can get along with the guy next door. We have to find some way to cooperate."

"We've really learned from BLADE RUNNER and BRAZIL," says production designer Iacovelli. "The problem with BLADE RUNNER or BRAZIL is you almost have to have an existentialist view of the future. While I'm not personally religious, the other thing I think adds a wonderful richness to the show is that these different societies have their own kind of religions. That's something they didn't deal with at all in STAR TREK, for some very obvious reasons, but it adds another kind of interest. You can't really deny a sort of shift in what our future view is. There was almost a paradigm shift when BLADE RUNNER came out, that the future isn't really going to be kelvinated refrigerator panels everywhere. That's my view of BABYLON 5 and director Richard Compton shares that view. He clued onto that very early on, and one of his first thoughts was that in the central corridor there should always be something that someone is fixing. There should constantly be a maintenance crew in the background gluing the ship back together. It's just like when you go downtown L.A. or anyplace in New York. To do justice to the look of N.Y. or L.A. in the 1990's you're going to have cones and red and white signs digging up the streets and fixing the infrastructure. That's what it looks like now. I think that's what the future is about a little bit. The other thing that we tried to do with BABYLON 5 is to give it a sense that it's not a brand new station, that it's been a little bit war-torn. It's like when you get on an L10-11 or 747 and you look out the window. The paint is sort of scratched off a little bit, the stuff doesn't quite fit together and all those plastic panels don't fit. It gives it a kind of texture and richness that makes it more realistic in a way and more accessible. Stuff just doesn't work perfectly and we tried to get that into BABYLON 5 because we feel that's a more realistic view."

Also helping Straczynski to visualize his future world is Visual Effects Supervisor Ron Thornton, who is responsible for the pilot's state of the art special effects--a revolution in computer generated imagery. Eschewing the use of miniatures and motion control cameras, every visual effect in the film (with the exception of Tamilyn Tomita) is designed using an elaborate system of Amiga computers, IBM's and Video Toasters.

"I was brought up on the generation that grew up on FIREBALL XL-5, STINGRAY, THUNDERBIRDS, LOST IN SPACE and, of course, Dan Dare," Thornton smiles. "I've never worked on anything like this in my life. It's really unique. We're not being that well paid, but you just want to do something that's really cool once in a while. I think people get pissed off with seeing too much pap on television. There's a lot of it about. Certainly in the past it's happened. You don't ask someone without a sense of humor to write a comedy show for you. Yet people will ask writers who don't know a damn thing about science fiction to write a science fiction show. I've never understood that, it just really goes against everything. But since when has Hollywood been logical?"

Straczynski agrees. "The producers often don't have the background in science-fiction, they don't know it and they don't want to know about science-fiction. They often view the genre with some creative contempt. When I was working as a journalist, I interviewed the producers of the "V" series. They said, 'If we have the sci-fi ray guns and starships blowing things up we'll get the science-fiction fans immediately, we have to go for the mainstream viewers," which is a really contemptuous thing to say. That's a part of it, the other is that science-fiction is mired in the 60's. It's like cop shows a long time before HILL STREET BLUES came along. It's the good guys being us, whether it's the Enterprise or the Galactica crew. There's no flaws in them whatsoever, and then there's the bad guys. There's not that much latitude you have in a show like that. Drama has progressed in television since the 60's and you have characters that are flawed and aren't one thing or the science-fiction hasn't caught up with that and I think if you merge those two aspects of a science-fiction premise combined with the characterization, writing and depth of HILL STREET or LA LAW, then you've got something."

BABYLON 5 graphic designer Ted Haigh concurs that science-fiction projects have been qualitatively bankrupt on television except for STAR TREK, a classic, which he hopes this show will supersede.

"I love STAR TREK, I love the series, we just want a slightly different tact. The genre is either Larry Niven-esque, totally science related science-fiction, or it's something where you can substitute the word dog for robot and it's hardly science-fiction at all. So the future is intrinsic to the plot, but the people are the most important aspect to show and as such it's been paralleled to ST. ELSEWHERE or HILL STREET BLUES in terms of the shooting and editorial styles."

In doing so, Straczynski, envisions a saga for television which will be traditionally episodic but have a larger story arc that tells an epic tale over the course of the proposed series run.

"The show's been in development for over four years and there are over 200 pages written by me for the five year storyline. What's important about the show is that each episode must stand individually -- but if you put it together a much larger story emerges and it builds towards that storyline. I know what basically happens in any given episode any of the seasons. I know what the last scene in the last episode in year five is going to be. I loved TWIN PEAKS desperately, but the problem was if you missed one show you were screwed. We want to set up things that pay off down the road but aren't so obscure you can't follow the show anymore."

The story of BABYLON 5 follows Captain Sinclair who, having played a mysterious role in saving the earth from destruction during a Minbari attack, is charged with running Babylon 5. This is the fifth of a series of space stations designed to play host to a series of galactic ambassadors representing the major warring alliances: the Earth Alliance, the Minbari, the Centauri, the Vorlons and the Narn Confederacy. As such, Babylon 5 serves as a intergalactic League of Nations, but more than that it is a catalyst for a vast array of stories involving treachery, humor, intrigue, espionage and romance. In creating this universal tapestry, Straczynski points to several of his favorite texts as thematic, if not narrative, inspiration.

"In terms of the characters, what's always appealed to me is sagas like LORD OF THE RINGS and the FOUNDATION books where one person's destiny affects countless others," says Straczynski. "In this story there's one character, Commander Sinclair, who has a destiny ahead of him. One of the three ambassadors is there for an enigmatic reason. Some say he is there to be his friend, some say he is there to kill him, some say both. They're both right. One of the ambassadors is watching Sinclair. If he goes this way, he's to help him. If he goes that way, he's to kill him. If he goes the right way there's a much broader tapestry. His existence is one of the reasons the war was stopped. There is something that was known about him that caused the Minbari to stop their attack on the earth."

In "The Gathering", Captain Sinclair is accused of poisoning the last ambassador to arrive on the station from the mysterious Vorlon regime, which could result in intergalactic war. Among the other questions Straczynski raises in the pilot that he promises answers to in the first season, are the mystery of Captain Sinclair's blackout while defending the earth and leading to the Minbari's surrender, what the alien Vorlons look like underneath their environmental encounter suits, and myriad other enigmatic aspects of the show set forth in the telefilm.

Ironically, the seed from which BABYLON 5 sprang was a short-lived science-fiction television show, CAPTAIN POWER & THE SOLDIERS OF THE FUTURE [Straczynski blames producer and MASTERS OF THE UNIVERSE director Gary Goddard for the inane SOLDIERS OF THE FUTURE tagline], which was stigmitized as a children's show. This was due to its affiliation with Mattel, who was producing toys, despite the show's mature science-fiction themes and impressive low-budget visuals. Straczynski, who served as series Story Editor, first met BABYLON 5 Executive Producer Doug Netter while they were bringing CAPTAIN POWER to life.

"We never intended CAPTAIN POWER for children," says Doug Netter. "We intended it for a more adult audience, but we could never overcome the fact that television stations would really be interested in only clearing early morning and weekend time periods because Mattel was involved. In this show, we have geared it for an adult prime time audience and I don't know if we learned from the other experience, but we certainly pinpointed the general audience: teenagers and families."

"It goes back to '86 or '87, having just come off one really expensive television show and seeing how it was run was nuts," Straczynski explains. "I said, 'Why can't you come up with a show that's creatively open but yet financially responsible?' You look at shows like HILL STREET BLUES or ST. ELSEWHERE, and what makes them interesting is you create a stable environment where you have your characters on their own turf and the stories come to them. When you're seeking out new life every week, your story becomes about that, rather than your characters which are never developed. This led me to a space station and, being a longtime CASABLANCA fan, I thought a free port like Spain in the 14th century would be a great setting where you have ships coming in from all over the world with refugees, diplomats, businessmen and slave traders."

In attempting to find an ally in the front offices of a major studio that would back the project, Straczynski and Netter approached several people with the fledgling series premise.

"We tried to go the foreign co-production route at first, which did not pan out," recalls Straczynski. "Then we went to Evan Thompson, the CEO of Chris-Craft Television. It's funny, when you talk to these guys they either get it or they don't get it -- and he got it immediately. He said work with me, we'll get this on the air somewhere."

Ultimately, Warner Bros. formed the Prime Time Entertainment Network, a loosely formed fifth network designed to deliver studio programming to independent stations in first-run syndication, with BABYLON 5 representing one of their flagship programs.

"While we were doing CAPTAIN POWER we were thinking about how great it would be to conceive a science-fiction show directly for television and that's what we did," says Doug Netter. "We were delighted to be able to present this to the TV consortium, which is now called the Prime Time Entertainment Network. They are beginning to program on a quality basis, so we've been allowed to make a film creatively the way we want to make it, backed by Warners. It's hard to believe that the same two men that we talked to close to five years ago are still involved and really the men behind the financing and distribution of the show."

While Paramount has sunk more money into DEEP SPACE NINE than even some feature films, Warner Bros. hasn't shown the same deep pockets, wary of an unproven commodity.

"Experience until recently with science-fiction shows has been very dangerous when it comes to control of costs," says Netter. "Some would immediately reject the project on the basis of cost control. There were others who said there's only a limited audience for science-fiction projects. We never believed that. The hardest obstacle to overcome was cost plus the feeling that if you do science-fiction for television the public is going to feel cheated because they don't see what they see with STAR WARS in a theatrical film. Many of the shows that were done after STAR WARS and until now have been shows that don't deliver the quality that a television audience wanted to see. But with today's advancement in technical achievement, we can avoid the disappointment of a television audience."

Warner Bros., reluctant to repeat their experience on "V", their last major science-fiction undertaking, which had gone wildly overbudget, agreed to produce the pilot and will take a wait and see attitude before approving production on the series. Ironically, it was Straczynski who penned the "V" revival script which would have returned the series to the airwaves for first-run syndication. However, when budget concerns rendered the project unviable, BABYLON 5 was picked up instead.

"If I didn't think there was enough money to do the show properly, I wouldn't do it," Straczynski emphasizes. "I feel strongly that a big problem in television is irresponsible producers who don't know how to work within a budget. "V" is an example of where they backed into a budget which was far beyond what they possibly could have done. I wanted to try to create a show that would be economical. I believe you should be responsible with other people's money, large amounts in particular. On MURDER SHE WROTE my shows always came in under budget because I worked with the production crew to see what we can and can't do. There's a point to prove with this show, first that we can do it within a reasonable budget and, secondly, with amazing quality."

In addition to the hard science-fiction element of the show, Straczynski promises some surrealism as well. "We're going to play with people's minds alot," he says. "What is real? What is not real? What is the individual? What is the role of society? Rather than making literary comparisons, I would say BABYLON 5 will have the action of the old

STAR TREK, the character of HILL STREET BLUES, and the surreal parts of THE PRISONER -- that's our show."

"We're making up the rules as we go along," says set designer Chris Muller. "We haven't been able to make this set and this set. We saw everything as pieces and make it into something else. Early on we were talking about going back to early science-fiction like Jules Verne, which you see in the central corridor. There's almost an Edwardian steel frame, as opposed to alot of science-fiction where the structure of a building is hidden and cleaned up like in STAR WARS or STAR TREK. Here, the external structure is on the inside. It's an early turn of the century feeling. Contemporary architecture, deconstructionist architecture, a lot of the materials are in conflict, metal against wood and John's used alot of raw wood which has made for an attractive and unusual look in science-fiction. There are no ground rules, it's total creativity."

The enthusiasm for the project shared by the entire crew includes its helmer, Richard Compton.

"He passed up two other jobs to come here, and without pay, start early on this thing and work with the cameraman and the production guys to get the look of this thing right," says Straczynski. "I've never seen that. He directed a whole bunch of EQUALIZER, HILL STREET BLUES and one STAR TREK, and vowed never to return. He was in an original STAR TREK as an actor and he's amazing. He agrees with me about the look of the show, which is we want to have a darker look. He wants to shoot it as you would a mainstream drama with all the shadows and textures. If you liked the look of THE EQUALIZER, that's what we're going to do on this."

"I love him," enthuses actress Patricia Talman, who portrays the telepathic member of the psi corps, Lyta, and starred in Tom Savini's remake of NIGHT OF THE LIVING DEAD and George Romero's KNIGHTRIDERS. "If you're doing what he wants you to do, he leaves you alone. He doesn't bother you. If he has a suggestion, you know he's right on. I got a sense of that as soon as I read for him. I really enjoy him, I compare him to George [Romero] and maybe that's why I'm comfortable with him. George was my first experience and I feel so comfortable with Richard."

Executive Producer Doug Netter has proposed an unorthodox directing roster for the show when it goes to series.

"I would like very much to have Richard join us with the series and if possible have him direct every other episode," says Netter of alternating directors bi-weekly (something the original STAR TREK attempted during its second season with Joseph Pevney and Marc Daniels). "If I could find two directors that are compatible, that's the best of all worlds. One prepares, one directs. We did it when I produced FIVE MILE CREEK in Australia and we changed the first assistant director, who stays with the director, because he can do budgets and overall production. It's prepare, shoot, prepare, shoot. It's wonderful continuity but you must have two directors who are just right."

Equally exciting and different from traditional science-fiction are the computer generated special visual effects which will be the first time such effects are utilized on a television science-fiction show.

"It does several things for us," says Straczynski. "We are allowed to do things on a scale previously unimaginable. The star gate's about 5-7 miles long and to create a model would be extremely expensive, as would the BABYLON 5 station. It allows us to put things in real perspective and we are always in perspective in the correct time ratios. It's more real than a model going by in front of a picture where the perspective isn't quite there. If you were going to have a dogfight, you could pick out one ship's point of view, that ship banks off, our pov changes to another ship, follows it around, move around and through the ship. You can start from 10 miles away and push through a window into a live action scene, and as you come through the window then hear the dialogue."

Ron Thornton points out that the special effects for BABYLON 5 done traditionally would cost over $2 million, more than the entire budget of the BABYLON 5 telefilm, but "[This is costing] considerably less."

For Straczynski, the production of BABYLON 5 is the culmination of a long-held dream.

"I've lived with this for four years in which time I could have sold alot of other stuff," Straczynski notes, "but I wanted to do a science fiction saga for television and the chance that this has finally come through is just a kick."

CHAPTER ELEVEN
Patrolling Deep Space:
Space Rangers

Another entry into the science-fiction sweepstakes this year is the six-episode limited series, SPACE RANGERS airing on CBS, a space opera from the production team behind BACKDRAFT and ROBIN HOOD: PRINCE OF THIEVES.

"Someone described us as a 'blue collar STAR TREK' but I think we're more in the RAIDERS OF THE LOST ARK/STAR WARS vein with a little bit of the ALIEN/ALIENS world than we are near STAR TREK," says series creator and Co-Executive Producer Pen Densham. "I think that what is going to distinguish us is the characters. I really like the characters we have, I think the people that are playing them are really breathing life into them."

The show's genesis is drawn from an idea that had been languishing on Densham's computer called PLANETBUSTERS, one of the many thoughts he had jotted down in the hopes of exploring further one day.

"Robin Hood was in my files for years as ROBIN HOOD ala RAIDERS," says Densham. "This was based, on a large degree, to see what happened when you parachuted a bunch of guys on a new planet and all the adventures that would engender."

Densham is quick to point out that he doesn't consider SPACE RANGERS a science-fiction show, but action adventure.

"I think that Asimov wrote science-fiction," says Densham. "Arthur C. Clarke writes science-fiction, Heinlein wrote action-adventure. I'm also a tremendous fan of Robert Sheckley and the way he sculpts characters and futuristic environments. I feel that the world that I'm trying to capture is one where it's more about the power of your ability to enjoy these worlds. I hate pure fantasy where it's knights and armors on a planet. That's too far to the right for me."

In fact, Densham prefers to liken his show to the romanticism of a World War II adventure film.

"I was very influenced by a lot of research I did on the Flying Tigers and the American Volunteer Group in 1942," says Densham. "There's a certain romanticism about that frontier where misfits and adventurers and people that believed that they had a mission in their own life, and women as well, went out there to the edges of a known civilization and plunked themselves down, and did it because of their beliefs. I tried to capture a lot of their emotions and instincts in SPACE RANGERS. That's why our ship has a shark drawn on it and why Chenault is named the leader of the group.

"It's all the wonderful things that as a kid your imagination would run away to," he continues. "In order to tell a continuing series of stories I tried to create a group of characters that paralleled World War II adventurers. I felt that was the last time we were romantic in a war environment and not skeptical, and it occurred to me the greatest way to focus an adventure series was to take the equivalent of a foreign legion fort and put it on the frontier. Instead of having a spaceship, have this milieu with the Arab Traders being present, and the various levels of civilizations from the hospitals to the cooks that were all present, and we could also launch out into the universe. That genesis started to happen."

The heart of SPACE RANGERS' futureworld is set at Fort Hope, an outpost of the Earth Confederacy on the edges of deep space. It is built on an ancient alien trading center races over the millennia have come to, and it's there that the Space Rangers protect Earth territory from a myriad of threats, including the Banshee, a violent and dire alien opponent.

"I wanted to have an unpredictable source of attack that we would later learn about and grow to actually admire," says Densham of the Banshees. "At the moment, they're the bad guys, we're at war with them, we are terrorized by them and treat them like savages. At some point, you're going to find out that, like the Apaches, they're actually intelligent and have a purpose, but that's way down the line."

In one episode, the Space Rangers find themselves on an abandoned spaceship commandeered by Banshees, where only one small boy has been left behind.

"Our guys have to go in and rescue him and Banshees can kill people in seconds," says Densham. "I asked that we put things into that ship you would never see in a television show. For instance, they go through several levels and on one level they have to wade up to their waist in water and fight Banshees. On most shows, there's no enthusiasm to work that hard, but we have an enormous number of effects and we're creating and learning as we go."

Jeff Kaake plays Captain Boon who, in the series opener, leads his crew to the forbidden world Skarrob, where they must rescue a former Space Ranger stranded there before the world's second sun rises and scorches the planet clean.

"It was just another audition in the beginning stages," explains Kaake, last seen in NBC's short-lived NASTY BOYS series. "But I really got into it after reading the script following the first or second audition. The character is a hero, which I've never played before. He's got to be real likable and have a good sense of humor. He's not just a Captain Kirk shouting orders. I want him to be very human. and I think they're really going to take the ball and run with it. He's whatever you would imagine a hero to be. He's a Harrison Ford/Mel Gibson hero, it's not Captain America. I want him to be real human and have good days and bad days.

"The one thing that did set the show apart immediately was how the cast gelled together from the very start," he adds. "It's unique to find six people who like to be around each other without conflict."

Also included among Boon's crew are newcomer Majorie Monoaghan as tough talking space pilot Jo Jo.

"If you play a strong woman, you either get a vamp siren who's very bitchy or someone who can't really pull it off," says Densham. "When we saw Majorie we realized there's an essential decency and innocence but at the same time there's a strength that we fell in love with. She has great strength and commitment and she never loses her femininity. We've asked her to slug guys and do all sorts of things. She's like Diana Rigg, she could do anything and never lose her charm."

Also on Boon's team of Space Rangers is a Grakka Warrior, played by Cary-Hiroyuki Tagawa, a fierce, cannibalistic warrior race which needs to have its animal passions subdued by an electronic pacifier.

"He's an extension of Azeem in ROBIN HOOD," says Densham, who co-wrote PRINCE OF THIEVES with his partner, Richard Lewis. "He's also very much an extension of Zulu from KING SOLOMON'S MINES and the strong silent Genghis Cook. I love Joseph Campbell mythology as a tool to try and understand what I do for a living. I think violence is inherent in the human animal and I think it's part of the alpha ape. When Kevin Costner was trying to get the woodsman to join up with him, he says what should I do, and I said 'Capture, don't lecture'. It's the same thing here. I think Cary and I have a lot of theories about what we're saying to the kids and we don't want them to know we're saying anything to them. We're saying you should be able to use all of your emotions, but you should be able to channel them. But we're not saying it in an obvious or preachy way. I think science fantasy or fantasy adventures are like fairy tales or parables in the sense that they put our people on quests that cause them to find things about themselves, which we can then look at and feel about ourselves. None of that should be done in a way in SPACE RANGERS where it gets too polemic or political or rigorously humanistic. Our guys are very humanistic, but not in a lecturing way."

Perhaps the biggest casting coup was that of Academy Award Winner Linda Hunt who plays Chenault, the commander of Fort Hope

"Chenault was written originally as a male and I said to my partner, Richard [Lewis], you're going to think I'm crazy," recalls Densham. "I expected a cynical laugh that I lost my senses when I said I really want Linda Hunt. He said that's a great idea. They sent the script to Linda and she came in and met with us. She's charming and intelligent and a tremendous actress, and her first question was it's a very nice script but I can't for the life of me figure out why you would want me for this role. She basically turned it back to me and said if you can explain it to me, I'll play it. Basically, I explained it to her. The pilot doesn't do her service. In the next batch of five episodes she just blossoms. She just gets stronger and stronger. She personifies a lot of things I want to say about the future. She has dedication and leadership without belligerence, and sensitivity without weakness."

Word of mouth has it that SPACE RANGERS really soars after its pilot, but one major aspect of the story that was changed after the filming of the premiere was the departure of Captain Boon's family--a wife and young daughter.

"I think it just opens up more story ideas if I'm single," says Kaake. "We're able to move around within storylines and it's easier for them to do the writing. The original idea was that Pen, and the whole group, come from such a moral background and had strong feelings in doing this show, that they wanted to have a moral in every story and have family issues and issues people deal with every day. That was the idea in having him married, and to go through all the battles of life we go through every day. But CBS also wanted this guy single, so his wife leaves him."

To bring his vision to the screen on a budget that Densham labels "considerably less than STAR TREK's", was one of the biggest challenges for the producer who turned to CGI, computer generated visual effects, to help create the look of the series.

"We hooked up with ILM because we had worked with them very closely on BACKDRAFT and the relationship had been very helpful to that movie," says Densham. "I didn't know anything about the lengths we could achieve with CGI. I heard of it and was willing to explore it and came at the special effects from the story base. As we went forward, we were toying with going with models and we came down to CGI as it became more and more real. We've now reverted to models in certain cases and CGI in others. There's a lot of R&D and there's different answers for every application. We're trying to spread out and work with a number of different groups that have the kind of creative instincts to challenge the limits of their technology. If someone has some special technique then I'd like to create a story around it. We'll build a starfield if we need to on the stage. The style I like is a lot of physical movement of the camera and I like a lot of lights. I'm just looking for energy and our shows have to be visually active. I don't want passive models, I want to try and get involvement and you really need to try different methods. The key is there's no one solution and it's being able to find the marriage of different ways of doing it. It's like KING KONG. There was a hand, there was a big one, there were little animated ones and it's basically breaking the story elements of the special effects into all those component elements so it appears seamless."

Of the Trilogy Entertainment team, actor Jeff Kaake opines, "It's one of the classiest acts I've seen during my tenure in Los Angeles. The combination of all three producers, Richard Lewis who's the driving force behind the group, and Pen being the creative one along with John [Watson]. They're very impressive people. The show has had a feeling of success from the day we started shooting."

Densham has high hopes for the future, when he feels the advances in computer technology will revolutionize the medium.

"I think we're still fairly primitive in terms of where we would like to be. If we're up and running for any period of time then I would like to see us working with ILM and a whole variety of people," says Densham. "We're at the cusp of an extraordinary change in technology. I think that we're still four years away from when it's going to get really extraordinary where we can create computer driven environments and characters. When you look at Nick Castle's THE LAST STARFIGHTER and saw that took a year to put those spaceships together and we're putting our spaceships together in CGI in a very short period of time, that speed-up is phenomenal. We're now able to sample images and bend flame around a circle and make a fire planet or take a wisp of the contrail of an F-16 and put that out of the back of a spaceship. You can literally do that movement. We don't have our Leonardo DaVincis in this world yet, we don't even have our Capras and our Von Sternberg's. That medium is going to create a whole new raft of video artists/storytellers and we're going to see worlds and creations using that storytelling medium which will be closer to the comic book format where you will put your characters into places which are quite extraordinary."

Contributing scripts to the series' first six episodes are STAR TREK veteran Herb Wright and BACKDRAFT scribe, Greg Widen. Says Densham, "I think television understimulates people's imaginations. There's a lot of room for shows that take people on adventures, and that *isn't* a rejection of our daily life. I'd say we're probably closer to the original STAR TREK which every week was a different bucket of popcorn. It was popping off the screen with new stuff and things you've never seen."

APPENDIX A.
The Critics Take On "DS9"

ENTERTAINMENT WEEKLY: "Viewers who don't know a Trekker from a Tribble may nevertheless be drawn into the orbit of STAR TREK: DEEP SPACE NINE, the latest, darkest, and densest TV STAR TREK yet. If the original TREK is the Old Testament of television science fiction and STAR TREK: THE NEXT GENERATION is New Testament, then DEEP SPACE NINE is the Apocrypha--mysterious variations on TREK lore that work as ripping tales in their own right.."

VARIETY: "....so what if DEEP SPACE NINE is not, like the first two TREK shows, a "Wagon Train to the Stars"? This latest TREK try need not be any more limited by its space-station setting than, say, GUNSMOKE was by its Dodge City setting. And perhaps GUNSMOKE-like durability is in store for NINE if producers, advertisers and the audience are willing to take the time to get to know a new crew and a new kind of TREK story. It will take some patience, but Paramount's latest TREK gamble can probably pay off as effectively as have the rest....The Berman-Piller script is a mixed bag, certainly too complex and ambitious at times, but generally admirable in its mix of deft characterization, old-fashioned space opera and sophisticated science-fiction concepts. As with NEXT GENERATION, the proper balance is by no means always achieved, but when it is, the result is commendable television...."

LOS ANGELES TIMES: "....Despite the guiding absence of the late Gene Roddenberry, who left the galaxy before the premise for the third live-action STAR TREK series was in place, this "S.T." is as pointedly P.C. as its message-heavy predecessors. But if tonight's solemn yet perky premiere is ample indication of its future pacing, there won't be much time for the show to get bogged down in its own progressive pontification. Fast and furious with exposition *and* Sci-Fi-losophy 101 expostulation, it may be the briskest two-hour TV pilot on record....Despite all the quantum metaphysics, there's no questioning the overriding hokum quotient in a show chock-full of such lines as 'I have been fighting for Bajoran independence since I was old enough to pick up a phaser!' So it ain't SOLARIS. It's soapy fun, flirts with actual ideas and has great stereo-surround effects during the explosions. Fasten your seat belts, it's going to be a bumpy 'Nine.'"

HOLLYWOOD REPORTER: "....[DEEP SPACE NINE] plays with visual and stylistic similarities to 'TNG' but in other ways it plays with a subtle different focus and interest.

And those subtle differences, combined with the impressive production values that continue from its big brother, are probably going to be just enough to make it work. It doesn't journey too far into worlds where no television show has gone before, but it comes with a personality and complexity not seen elsewhere and it proves a pleasing combination. 'Emissary' is a little confusing in some spots as the show's premise is established, but it's also quite exciting. It's a well-made, well-acted program that goes somewhat beyond the usual limits of sci-fi in that here the space travelers find themselves a home. The film comes complete with fantasy sequences and spiritual realities that are a kick, and is filled with flashbacks and a kind of non-linear construction that both gives this show a fitting texture and helps propel this series and the characters into the future and away from its predecessor....With a start like this, it will be hard for DEEP SPACE NINE not to hit."

NEW YORK DAILY NEWS: "There are two ways to look at STAR TREK and its offspring, of which it has more than a mayfly. Either it's the greatest idea since tossed salad or it gives you a headache the size of Nova Scotia. So it should come as no surprise that STAR TREK: DEEP SPACE NINE....will delight the fans and not disturb the slumber of the rest.....Like all STAR TREK scripts, this one dabbles heavily in cosmic philosophizing. It also dabbles heavily in symbolism--like the way tribal factions of Bajor begin fighting each other after the evil invading Cardassians finish their looting and pull out. Does this sound like post-Soviet Eastern Europe to you, boys and girls? The cast of DEEP SPACE NINE seems sturdy. They should stay employed for awhile."

MARK A. ALTMAN (CINEFANTASTIQUE writer and co-author of EXPLORING DEEP SPACE....AND BEYOND): "'Emissary', the DEEP SPACE NINE pilot, exceeds expectations and is far more dramatically compelling than the comparatively ponderous 'Farpoint' launch of the new TREK series progenitor, STAR TREK: THE NEXT GENERATION, six years ago. Substituting top-heavy mystical New Age mumbo jumbo for the familiar scientific technobabble, writer Michael Piller aims for the cerebral resonance of the best moments in 'The Cage,' but 'Emissary' is not always a success in that regard. Its first hour is top-notch TREK establishing the premise of the new series and introducing an intriguing array of new characters sparked by a powerful teaser in which Sisko (Avery Brooks) faces Picard as Locutus at Wolf 359.

"However, the film's second hour is considerably less involving as it grows mired in Sisko's metaphysical journey into his "pah." The opener suffers from the same problems plaguing ST: TNG's premiere with an impressive first hour and a disappointing second half. The mystical and metaphysical have no place in the rational and secular world of STAR TREK, and by giving credence to the Bajorans' religious beliefs it weakens a strong area of conflict between the humanist crew and the spiritual Bajorans.

"DEEP SPACE works best while exploring the decks of Deep Space Nine and becomes lost in space once Sisko begins his mystical journey. The prophet's exploration of linear existence often becomes convoluted and tiring and reduces the quickly unfolding plot to a lethargic crawl. The pilot is also, at times, somewhat dour and humorless. The exceptional tech credits often compensate for some of the script failings, including terrific work by Robert Blackman with costumes, Herman Zimmerman and his outstanding team of production designers and a new level of proficiency on the part of Rob Legato and his visual effects maestros, which have redefined the state-of-the-art for televised special effects. The film's landing pad and shuttle effects, including a lifepod launched from the Saratoga during the telefilm's teaser, are particularly impressive as are the design of the station itself by Herman Zimmerman.

"Unquestionably, Piller's pilot script services some of the characters better than others. Making the most impressive mark is Nana Visitor as Kira Nerys, who is willful and strong and effortlessly segues between sarcasm and self-assurance. It's a competent and promising performance which illustrates that the role of women in the 24th century is finally being accorded with the proper respect by not relegating the actress to caretaker duties. Equally promising is Armin Shimerman as Quark, who is the most fully realized Ferengi character STAR TREK has ever achieved. While retaining the familiar Ferengi qualities of lasciviousness and deceit, Quark is a cross between Peter Lorre and Sidney Greenstreet in CASABLANCA, and Shimerman successfully reigns in the broadest tendencies associated with portraying a member of this race. It's a tribute to his thespian skills that he is able to make a Ferengi palatable as a regular member of the TREK ensemble.

"Avery Brooks invests his role of Benjamin Sisko with the proper mix of pathos and strength, although there is a certain degree of monotonous theatricality to his take on the role which will hopefully diminish as Brooks becomes more comfortable with the rigors and demands of acting in STAR TREK. Regardless, Brooks certainly holds his own with guest star Patrick Stewart, which is no mean feat for any actor. Brooks seems poised to assume the mantle of leadership which has been established by William Shatner and Stewart in past star treks.

"As for the rest of the ensemble, the jury's still out. Terry Farrell, whose background is in modeling, gives a promising performance and brings an unexpected degree of irreverence to her role as Dax, the Trill. Of course, to watch Terry Farrell read the phone book would be captivating enough, but she promises to continue to develop into one of the most interesting members of the ensemble. Rene Auberjonois is professional and enigmatic, as the role of Odo calls for, although the danger remains of the shape-changing gag becoming an overused cliché, but Auberjonois' acerbic detachment makes this more than the Data-derived character the role was initially pegged as by TREK pundits. Colm Meaney isn't given much to do and his departure from the Enterprise lacks the emotional punch of De Kelley's cameo in "Farpoint"--certainly the lack of Keiko and the other Enterprise regulars in the pilot is a detriment to O'Brien's development in the opener.

"Most disappointing is Siddig El Faddil as Dr. Bashir, and it's through no fault of his own. He is portrayed as naive and, at times, plain stupid. Faddil is never given the chance to shine and is instead embarrassed and harangued at every turn. Faddil promises to become one of the strongest and most interesting members of the ensemble, though "Emissary" fails to showcase the character of this charismatic actor in a positive way.

"The two-hour opener's other major disappointments are a thoroughly unremarkable new title theme, courtesy of Dennis McCarthy, whose music for the show has never been memorable (reportedly Jerry Goldsmith didn't turn in the main title music which had been commissioned from him on time). The lack of the familiar STAR TREK theme is a particular misstep, although one suspects it was to avoid paying royalties to Alexander Courage. The telefilm's opening titles are also somewhat cheesy, primarily because of the weak post-production integration of video titles with the original film, and the endless beauty passes of the station becoming monotonous--making the endless drydock sequence in STAR TREK: THE MOTION PICTURE Look downright exciting in comparison.

"Regardless of its flaws, 'Emissary' offers every indication that DEEP SPACE NINE has the potential to be the best of the STAR TREK shows yet with one of the best casts and most intriguing ensemble of characters conceived so far. With a healthy budget being provided by Paramount along with the strong pool of directing and writing talent assembled by TREK honchos Piller and Berman, DEEP SPACE NINE should truly go where no STAR TREK has gone before."

APPENDIX B.
DIRECTING "DEEP SPACE"
by Edward Gross

An Interview With David Carson

David Carson has certainly left his mark on the STAR TREK universe, having helmed such important NEXT GENERATION episodes as "Redemption" (part two), "The Enemy" and one of the most popular ever, "Yesterday's Enterprise." Not surprisingly, given the general tone of his episodes, Carson was asked to direct the pilot of DEEP SPACE NINE, "Emissary."

"I have the feeling that the darker, grittier tone is one of the reasons they wanted me to direct the pilot. They want my experience with grit in STAR TREK. It is true that this will be a much grittier environment than the Enterprise, which is part of the attraction. And it's my feeling that that part of the grittiness of DEEP SPACE NINE is not only the setting, but the attempt to access the slightly weaker side of human nature, while still telling extremely powerful and insightful stories. Perhaps the most striking thing about DEEP SPACE NINE is the immense strength of the two-hour movie's storyline, which has a universality that is quite striking. "

Q: In taking on the first episode of a new branch of the STAR TREK franchise, it must be a considerable challenge.

A: Wonderfully challenging and very interesting because you've got a lot of people you mustn't let down. But it's a good challenge. Unlike a lot of shows where you're sort of stabbing in the dark, here you have a lot of background. I think if they had decided to make major departures from the way everything had been, it may have been a different kettle of fish. Because the producers made sure they were sticking very clearly to Gene Roddenberry's mapped-down path, then we were really continuing the inheritance as it were. My job as director rather than as a writer is to make it look better, be better, be bigger, be more effective, communicate better than it had before.

Q: I guess it's the trick of taking it further than it's gone before, without losing sight of the elements that made the show popular in the first place.

A: I think so, though I think the story went a long way beyond where STAR TREK normally goes. The decision was made *not* to pander to new audiences, but to play to the strengths of the STAR TREK audience. So the story doesn't take any prisoners. If you're not on that wavelength, then I think there are a lot of people who may have been confused by it a little bit. But if you have the patience to sit with it, then I think it all becomes completely clear as to what's going on.

Q: So rather than comment, "Oh, we're on the holodeck," you just use it without explanation on the show. Or when Picard is depicted as Locutus.

A: Exactly. Similarly when the aliens appear as memories, nobody says to the audience, "Hey guys, these are aliens that we're dressing up." You just let them talk and eventually the audience will understand what's going on. It seems to be that that's a good way to approach it, because it treats the audience--the entire audience, not just the TREK audience--with a great deal more intelligence. You don't have to hammer it over the head or spell it out, which everyone seems to think you have to for American audiences. I'm one of those people who believes that the audience is very much more intelligent than television people give them credit for. And in this sort of thing, letting them discover things as they go along and letting their natural intelligence come to bear on the subject, actually gives you a much richer TV program than you would otherwise have. I think that's what we were trying to do, and certainly when we were shooting it that's what we had in mind.

Q: As the director of the pilot, what would you say your greatest contribution to DEEP SPACE NINE was?

A: It's very difficult to quantify. I think we made tremendous efforts in the two-hour show to put a lot of production value on the screen to make it seem not like a TV movie, but a really big, thunderous movie that you would sit in the movie house and see. And to give it a feeling of scale and complexity in the way that we shot it and the way that I directed the actors. It gives the audience the feeling that they're not just watching some other TV sequel, but that they're watching a movie. It's my feeling that TV needs to try and harness a lot more of the qualities of movies because they're up against so many on cable TV and everywhere else. That's what we strove to do during that time.

Q: You mention scale. From the first moment until the Saratoga explodes after being fired upon by the Borg, and you've got the reflection of the explosion over Sisko's face, you get the feeling that you're watching something along the lines of STAR WARS in terms of scale.

A: I think it was intended to have as large a scale as we could in the beginning so that you were propelled into the film with a lot of interest and a lot of information to assimilate and absorb, and let it unravel from there. We were also conscious that since the opening is such a terrific whiz-bang affair and because the show is quite complex, we didn't want to hurtle all the acting and dialogue along at the usual television speed, which is sort of like 90 miles per hour, but to give it some consideration and let the characters develop and expand. And allow the thing to have a little more cinematic time rather than wall-to-wall dialogue. In fact, when we finished shooting it we discovered that the whole thing was twenty minutes too long and we had to take twenty minutes out of it.

Q: Really? What did you lose?

A: [laughs] Some really nice stuff.

Q: Anything in particular come to mind?

A: No, there were just other scenes, complex ideas which helped the main idea. I think if you seen it with these additional twenty minutes, I don't think anyone would have said, "My goodness, it's twenty minutes too long." It's one of those things where maybe someday those extra twenty minutes will be put back in and the texture will be much richer and slightly more accessible than they otherwise might have been.

Q: Were you involved with the casting of the main characters?

A: Completely.

Q: Was that a tough process? After all, this was the first time they were casting a STAR TREK series without Gene Roddenberry's involvement, and Roddenberry was adamant in the press that he was the only person who could successfully cast STAR TREK.

A: It was a very long and torturous process, but I think the cast we came up with in the end was very good.

Q: Was there any character tougher to cast than any other?

A: I think the most difficult part to cast was Sisko, because that character is taking over the traditional role of Captain Kirk and Jean Luc Picard. Whoever plays that part is going to be the sort of standard-bearer for the next several years, because I don't think anybody doubts that this series is going to run as long as the others did. I mean THE NEXT GENERATION's market-share at the moment is, I think, twelve, and it kicked off at seven.

Q: And I've heard that the show has been renewed for two more years, *without* Patrick Stewart.

A: He may reappear for a couple of guest shots. Quite honestly, I don't think it will effect the show at all.

Q: Why would you say that? It seems impossible to believe that it won't.

A: I believe that the show is not about a star and not about a Captain Kirk or a Jean Luc Picard. I think there will inevitably be some sort of shake-up, as there always is when a captain leaves a ship, and there will be a feeling of the ground. But you may find that you get a different, richer NEXT GENERATION out of it and you're not simply retreading the same waters with the same people. The regrouping of the cast and the realignment of the actors towards either new people or redistribution of their own strengths, will inevitably make THE NEXT GENERATION different.

Q: One assumes that Riker will take over the Enterprise.

A: I don't know, I've been working completely on DEEP SPACE NINE, so I'm out of the loop. But if he does, that gives you a different type and, after six years, a richer way of going, because you've got all that information from six years and now you can take it in a different way with a different personality. It has to be good for the show because unlike ROSEANNE, the show does not depend on one actor. In fact it's very much the opposite. I think it will become much more interesting without him. Not that that means I have no respect for Patrick Stewart, but if I was running that show I would be delighted at the opportunity of having to deal with not having that character in it. To me he's not the star of the show. The whole cast is. If you lose one component the others will regroup and the show will continue because it's much stronger than its individual actors or characters.

Q: Moving back to DEEP SPACE NINE, NEWSWEEK commented on the fact that a black actor being given the lead role in such a series was revolutionary, following the somewhat stereotypical all-American hero characterizations previously established.

A: As an Englishman, I'm not very qualified to comment on that. I do know that we decided that the role could be played either by a white man or a black man, or as in the case of Picard by an American or Englishman, or Belgian or German. In fact we did interview a Belgian actor and a German actor who came over from England. What race or creed he was was very important, but it was never a question of whether or not there were opportunities for everyone, every type of person to play the role. In the end, even though you would expect us to say this, I think all of us can quite truthfully say that we were able to come down to what we considered to be the best actor for the job. I think that Avery Brooks is a phenomenal actor. I've rarely come across an actor with a combination of his incredible depth of ability to portray emotions and feelings, but also his extraordinary technical skill in front of the camera and an amazing strength of performing with the lens. He's a real joy to work with. And the way he senses out the character.....We've now done ten episodes and I directed the eighth and the tenth, and he has developed his character now beyond "The Emissary" into a very subtle blend of types of feeling and the way he handles himself in different situations. He's extraordinarily deft and constantly interesting, and I think the character gives him much more ability to have these differences in his psychological make-up than Picard, who's a much more straight-forward character who you can probably predict will react in different situations. It's very difficult to do that with Sisko, and Avery plays with delight those opportunities.

Q: One of the casting moves that surprised me was that of Odo, Rene Auberjonois, who I've known primarily from his stint on BENSON.

A: Like Avery, Rene has this extraordinary classical background. He, like Avery, is a classically trained stage actor. Both of them have come out of this tradition of performance. So to have the luxury of someone like Rene Auberjonois playing a shape-shifter is quite extraordinary, because he isn't really first and foremost a TV actor who comes out of BENSON. He's a guy with this huge, long history of the performing arts. Although many people know him for who he was in BENSON. He has turned this character into somebody absolutely fascinating. And the fact that he is classically trained makes him particularly able to work with this mask-like thing that's on his face. He's an actor who's learned how to work with and through a mask because he's trained with masks and, I think, trained other people to act with masks. You get much more richness and depth out of somebody like him than somebody who doesn't have that depth of experience.

Q: What are you feelings regarding Nana Visitor?

A: The cast and company is so lucky to have her. She's one of these rare chameleon kind of actors who is able to assimilate herself into a character and transform it into something you don't expect. She's also very beautiful and she obviously delights in playing this role. I was very pleased when she walked into the room and I think that once she did, she was the only Kira that we thought could play the role. Of course we weren't going to tell anybody that until we'd signed a deal with her [laughs]. She was and is extraordinary. She's also delightful to work with and she's able to tune her emotions to the camera. She also has this specific, tangible relationship with the lens, which is delightful for a director to work with.

Q: Was the character a tough one to cast?

A: Yes, it was. Though no more so than when you're setting up something completely new because on these television things everything is done by committee. So you're juggling three million opinions at the same time. It's sort of a different world from the one that I'm used to in that sense. You feel as though you're walking through a minefield as you struggle towards the final choice in television, it seems to me, because there are a whole mixture of opinions to be taken into account, some informed and some uninformed. Sometimes, as we all know, terrible mistakes happen in casting. I think, though, we were extremely lucky this time and everybody had the necessary patience to not say yes because we had to start shooting. In fact some of the roles weren't cast until we were three weeks in to it. We had to change the schedule around to accommodate it. With a show like this getting a good cast is really so important.

Q: Oh sure. You have to make it believable for the audience. If you don't have believable people in the roles....

A: Yes, and it's an immensely strong and talented cast.

Q: How about Terry Farrell as Dax?

A: She's excellent. She was one of the ones cast very late. Most of the time with her was struggling to see what in fact a Trill should look like. Together with the fact that she was cast very late, we had all these problems of what should be stuck on her face. There were countless tests and some people didn't like this, some people didn't like that until eventually she came out with spots. I don't know if you know this, but Trills have an established look which is a sort of lumpy prosthetic look on their faces. As you'll notice, she in fact doesn't have any. When we first started shooting her she had these old prosthetic lumps on her face. But frankly they did not add to her undeniable attractiveness and so everybody decided that her face should be left alone and spots should be added which went under the collar of her costume, thereby being suggestive of where else the spots might be. Not that anybody will *ever* know [both laugh].

Q: Come on, give us an "R" rated version.

A: Think of the make-up time it would take.

Q: Let's move to Armin Shimerman as Quark.

A: Armin and I worked together on another science-fiction show called ALIEN NATION. Armin is terrific. Like Rene, he has taken to the mask completely and is developing his character wonderfully well. Unlike some of the Ferengi characters there have been, Quark is not quite so silly as some of them. He has a much more malevolent presence, which I think is very good because it adds to the drama. He's, again, delightful to work with, extremely able technically and in all other ways.

Q: It's interesting that Armin used to be on BEAUTY AND THE BEAST, where Ron Perlman was made up as Vincent. I would imagine Armin has a lot of empathy for Perlman now.

A: I think so. He's a very patient man. Everybody knows when they buy into this show that's what it's going to be, you're going to spend hours in a make-up chair. But such is the enthusiasm for the show, that everybody buys into it completely. I mean, Michael Dorn's been doing it for several years now.

Q: Siddig El Faddil. as Dr. Julian Bashir.

A: What a wonderful actor he is, freshly minted from British drama school. A very wonderful candor and openness of feeling about him. And for such a young actor, very experienced with the lens. Very good at turning his hand to all the tricks of the emotions the writers have asked of him so far. He's, again, a wonderful addition to the team and it's great that he comes from England, but of course I would think that [laughs].

Q: Colm Meaney, who has transferred over from NEXT GEN as O'Brien.

A: I've worked with him before on NEXT GENERATION and he's tremendous. Very wonderful, warm, interesting, varied actor, and I think it's an interesting choice to have him come over from NEXT GENERATION. He wasn't particularly prominent over there and to suddenly reveal him is a good way of linking the two series together without doing it heavy-handedly. I think that's a really good choice.

Q: I've got to tell you, though, there were a couple of moments there where he really sounded like Scotty.

A: [laughs] Maybe the tradition lives on!

Q: Cirroc Lofton as Sisko's son, Jake.

A: A very, very talented young man. He had minimal drama training, according to his mother, and for a boy who's had so little training, he's really quite good. He was way and above the best actor that we saw for the role, and we saw many, many actors. I think he has a refinement of manner and a refinement of feature as well, which makes him just that little bit set apart, which I think is very good for Sisko's son. His family comes from Ethiopia and I suppose his background has had some effect on him, his bearing and how he looks. But I think he's very bright and has a big future. He's the new Wesley.....

Q: Don't say that [both laugh]. Do not categorize it like that!

A: Unfortunately one tends to. The thing about Cirroc is that he's growing so fast now that we're doing the series. We're not quite sure when he's going to overtake Avery.

Q: Do you have a favorite among these characters?

A: I don't really. I like working with them all in different ways. You get to be very intimate with a cast when you do a pilot with them. With this you and they are creating the basis of their series sailing off into the future. So it becomes a very intense and intimate relationship. Mine with them is equally shared. I enjoy working with them all equally, and I enjoy the characters that they're making a lot. In the past, in THE NEXT

GENERATION, my personal favorite among all the types of people there have been are Klingons and there's no regular Klingons on Deep Space Nine yet.

Q: Earlier we had talked about the opening of the pilot, and one thing I noticed--and I mean this in a good way--is that you went Steadicam crazy with it.

A: As a matter of fact it wasn't the Steadicam. It was a brand new device called the Aaton hand-held camera, which is an incredibly light. It's brand new on the market, and it has the ability to be underslung, which means you don't have to keep your eye to the eyepiece. There's a video feed that sits on top of the camera, and it's specifically designed to be hand held. Steadicam is such a cumbersome thing to use in the tight spaces I was in and you very often can't use Steadicam and use the long lenses that I like. Discovering this camera, which I used extensively during the pilot, was a great thing to have on board.

Q: It just brought you right into the action.

A: You can really use it very well and we of course have a wonderful camera crew that can handle these things well. We also used a great deal of remote-control camera on a crane and a dolly, which enabled us to get into all sorts of corners we couldn't otherwise get in to. Which of course you can do when you're doing a two-hour pilot.

Q: I assume that from the beginning there was a very conscious effort to differentiate DEEP SPACE NINE from the look and tone of THE NEXT GENERATION.

A: That's true.

Q: Was that difficult after all these years of NEXT GEN, or something looked forward to?

A: It was something I think everyone looked forward to. The feeling on THE NEXT GENERATION is one of such cleanliness, a smoothed down Holiday Inn type of thing, that it was great feeling you were going into a grubby space station that didn't work, was alien, wasn't properly lit, was dark and gloomy, and I think that was something that the DP particularly seized upon. I think the grittiness and difference of approach paid off.

Q: When you went to that scene with Sisko and Picard on the Enterprise you had to shift gears, you're back in this Club Med environment yet there's this tension there that's so unusual for the Enterprise.

A: Absolutely, you don't get that sort of tension between Starfleet officers, so for people who have watched the series before it's a really weird scene because these guys are not sort of smiling, grinning, shaking hands and seeming all buddy-buddy. One of them hates the other and the other sees that there's justification for his hatred.

Q: Speaking of relationships on the show, one thing I noticed during the pilot was the snapping between Quark and Odo. Has this developed into a Spock/Bones type relationship during the ensuing episodes?

A: In a way, but not so specifically because it's not like they're on the same spaceship. Odo has Quark's bar under his eye and he and Quark come into contact from time to time, but it's a very different sort of situation. Maybe you're right, but I'm not as acquainted with that first series as well as I should be. I think it will be interesting to see how the relationship between them develops.

Q: Did you enjoy the allegory the story took regarding Europe, the Middle East, etc.?

A: I think if you can draw parallels to things it's absolutely wonderful, because people make the inferences for themselves without you hitting them over the head. I think that so often people turn off their TVs because everything is being preached to them. But, again, if you give audiences an allegory or parable and let them draw their own inferences, if they want to see Bosnia in it then good for them because it's done its work for them on that level. If they don't, then equally good for them because it does its work on another level. I think if you can entertain first but include all sorts of different messages to people in different ways, that's wonderful. To many people it must have meant a great deal on its base, emotional level about grief and leaving grief behind. How you deal with that sort of thing. The number of people who watched it who have been in that situation--most of us have lost a loved one--and to watch it spelled out in that way, gives you a chance to relate to it in a way you can't if you're listening to a psychiatrist or some guy on a chat show telling you what you really ought to be doing or feeling. You're able to step back and observe it. It's like having a song sung to you or a poem read to you where you can relate to the imagery with whatever perceptions you as a viewer bring to it, which is the same as looking at a painting. I don't mean to be pompous about it, but I think it has a lot of interesting elements inside it which is what makes it good and a cut beyond much of what is seen on TV.

Q: The mystical, spiritual elements of the show was very surprising, because that, again, is not something STAR TREK normally deals with.

A: I think there was a deliberate attempt made to make those differences and to let emotions and mysticism and spirituality and those sorts of words which are never normally attached to STAR TREK, and probably people would deny they're there, but they are definitely within this show. There was an effort made to let them blossom whereas under normal circumstances in THE NEXT GENERATION era they would not have been allowed to see the light of day. From that level down to basic things like O'Brien kicking the transporter panel. You don't see *that* in NEXT GENERATION.

Q: One of the criticisms I've gotten from people regarding that first episode is that Sisko's trying to relate to these aliens the nature of linear existence slows things down and seems to dilute the other half of the story regarding the Cardassians and Deep Space Nine itself; that it seems like two separate ideas were grafted together.

A: I actually thought of it as another interesting parallel. Inevitably you have people who want to see more action than philosophy going on. But it seems to me that the first two-hour story is about a man coming to grips with a loss, a terrible, terrible loss in his life. That's the main story and it's set against the Federation taking over a space station outside Bajor and then the Cardassians. The two stories are joined by the spiritual elements of the Orbs, where they actually lead Sisko to discover himself. In fact, I think that the two stories join together. In a way it's good that it isn't a linear development. In many of the great stories of the world, like for example WAR AND PEACE, you have two entirely different chunks going along at different paces. I rather enjoyed the fact that you were in one area where Sisko is desperately telling these people that he's dealing with something that was violent to himself but was also telling them that we are not a threat to you; we as a linear people value life more than anything else. Then in the other storyline you've got people beating the shit out of each other, which completely negated what he was saying. It's true. We have an idea of ourselves as humans that we value life more than anything else, but we don't practice it. So that was the idea of that parallel imagery going on in that story.

Q: The Cardassians as villains seem to be growing in popularity. They seem to be showing up more and more.

A: They're the Nazis of the universe. They're quite cunning and sly. They're wonderful political antagonists, which I think is well set up in the scene between Sisko and Gul Dukat.

Q: Right, Gul Dukat saying, "It wasn't that long ago that I was sitting on that side of the table."

A: Exactly, the two of them fencing with each other. So they're good antagonists.

Q: "Emissary" was much more special effects heavy than an episode of NEXT GEN. Is it difficult dealing with so much post production work?

A: If there's the time to do it, then the answer is no. The impact it has on the director is that you have to make sure that what you shoot--if all the special effects are going to be shot afterwards--is completely in synch with what the visual effects people shoot. And the way that you intend the bits and pieces to go together and come together. Quite frankly sometimes disasters come about because not enough attention is paid to that. Special effects are done at the wrong pace or cut in from the wrong angle, or you leave a cut with one guy going one way and then the spaceship comes into frame from the wrong side, which gives the audience an unnecessary jolt. But because we had a long time to prepare this, we were able to put our heads together a great deal and make sure we were in synch. We used storyboards and other aids to help us map the scenes out. When I finished the principal photography, all the areas we had to slot into the show after that had been well covered and we proceeded relatively easily. It's only a question of planning. It seems to me that it's only overwhelming if it isn't properly planned and if it hasn't been properly worked out before hand. If you come upon it later you say, "My God, what are we going to do here?" and you treat visual effects as a band-aide that's going to make the whole thing work after you finish shooting, then you're in deep trouble. If you leave it to the end, you cannot possibly get as good a result no matter how good your effects are than if you had planned it at the beginning.

There was also a tremendous amount of looping as well because of all the special things. There were burning quarters, even scenes we did on the beach. I wanted a high sea in the background but the pounding of the waves drowned out the dialogue, so you get all these conflicts between sound and picture which on normal television you cannot have that conflict. On these things you can make sure that the picture has all the qualities in it that you need, even though those qualities--like fire and water--make a lot of noise which interferes with the dialogue. Again, fortunately, Avery and the rest of the company have proven themselves to be utterly brilliant at looping and laying in dialogue afterwards.

Q: If you had to categorize them, how would you say NEXT GENERATION and DEEP SPACE NINE are similar and different?

A: It's difficult to say. If you accept that they're in the same time and the same universe, with the same beliefs and created by the same people, you then come down to the basic and most obvious differences. THE NEXT GENERATION is a story about people on a starship which finds its adventures wherever it's sent or stops, whereas DEEP SPACE NINE is static, basically, apart from a few thrusters which move it around a bit. The adventures have to come to the space station. That is its main difference. Therefore, the people are not wonderfully set up to get along with each other. There's also this awful mixture of people who are all muddled up together on this space station whether they like it or not. Then you have the fact that the Starfleet characters on DEEP SPACE NINE are far more emotional and prone to emotions and philosophy and religious and mystical experience and those sorts of things which are closer to our perception of human life and behavior than the Starfleet officers of THE NEXT GENERATION, who are by and large not subject to conflict between them. The series' strength is that they behave in a way that is utterly correct and unconflicted towards each other. It's Gene Roddenberry's 24th century.

Q: What would you say the difference is between helming a two-hour premiere and the one hour installments?

A: About ten million dollars [both laugh]. Once you're running in a series it's a lot easier than the pilot. Doing a pilot is an enormously difficult and challenging thing. I can't think of a TV show that I've seen which is as complex as this. Just putting the thing together and imagining this world and everything that went into it, was immensely complex. Doing the episodes is something of a relief after that.

Q: For you, which home is more comfortable in the 24th century, NEXT GENERATION or DEEP SPACE NINE?

A: I feel equally at home on both of them. DEEP SPACE NINE is the new show so therefore it is more challenging and interesting to develop because you are constantly developing it as with any new show. However, THE NEXT GENERATION has very good stories, characters that I feel very at home with and people on it who I respect a great deal and enjoy working with. It's a 24th century toss-up.

An Interview With Winrich Kolbe

Director Winrich "Rick" Kolbe has been involved with STAR TREK since season two's "Where Silence Has Lease." Since then he has helmed "Pen Pals," "Up the Long Ladder," "Evolution," "The Bonding," "Allegiance," "Galaxy's Child," "Identity Crisis," "Darmok," "The Masterpiece Society," and "Cost of Living." He is one of a handful of directors that Rick Berman and Michael Piller have chosen to helm episodes of their newest creation, STAR TREK: DEEP SPACE NINE.

Q: One thing that immediately comes to mind upon watching "Past Prologue" is the level of politics at play on DEEP SPACE NINE, so unlike THE NEXT GENERATION.

A: I like it. I think in the last interview we had we talked about one of my major problem areas is the lack of conflict within the group itself on TNG. Now we have a show where there is conflict within the group, which is partially caused by the fact that we basically have a benevolent occupational force sitting on DS9 in the name of Starfleet, which is basically running affairs to a certain degree, I would say, on the planet Bajor. It is an area that has just been recently liberated from the Cardassians, so there are a lot of things going on politically which we'll explore as the episodes come down the pike.

Q: You mention conflict, but there's also frailties within the characters. For instance, in "Past Prologue" Bashir is so nervous and uptight and gullible about this Cardassian Garick.

A: I don't think you would have a character like Bashir on TNG. They are a lot more advanced on TNG, emotionally more stable which is something I feel might be a detriment to TNG. But, again, I'm one person and there are millions who are perfectly happy with the world as it is in TNG.

Q: Now that we're getting a taste of what it could be like in terms of conflict, I think people are going to race to this show.

A: Hopefully they do. Hopefully it will explore, to a large degree, a new audience, because I don't want TNG to suddenly be left alone, which I don't think will happen. There are die-hards who will look at TNG as a different approach to storytelling than DS9.

Q: Do you prefer allegory tales to straight science-fiction or drama?

A: I don't want to make a statement that makes it sound as though I prefer those in exclusivity. They have their place and it's very important. Writers have been dealing with contemporary problems in terms of futuristic allegories for centuries. But it's got to be done intriguingly; in a new way. I feel that sometimes just to throw in an allegory because it's kind of poppish is not doing it any service. It just gets buried. But to deal with certain issues that we would have a problem dealing with on a present-day level is something that, yes, I support very, very strongly.

Q: What are your feelings regarding the Cardassians as villains?

A: You know, there are certain shows on TNG that I always thought I would like to do. Number one, these are the shows where somebody or the whole group goes into the holodeck and it turns into 19th century Victorian England. I've never done a Klingon show, I've never done a Cardassian show. I don't know if it's coincidence or somebody sits up there and says, "We don't want Rick Kolbe for this show because his strengths are in another area." I doubt it because those poor guys pushing out the scripts don't know which directors are coming down, they just have to have a script. So my first encounter with a Cardassian was in the DS9 show. Having said that, I think we would all agree that the Cardassian in this episode was not symbolic of the Cardassians in general. They're supposed to be a very war-like race, and they are the main threats to DS9 at this particular time. They're intriguing because they are different, but what intrigues me more is the attitude of Sisko. He seems to be, in a way, glumly defending the point of view of Starfleet, which is don't screw around with them. But you also have the feeling that the Cardassians know that he is the power of the land, so "Don't screw around with me."

Q: Certainly the general tone between the two series is different.

A: I've been thinking about it, and I'm more intrigued by DS9 right now. That could be because I've done one show and I'm just prepping the second one, and it's new. The sets are new, the actors are new, the storylines are new. I'm not sure whether or not I'm reacting to the newness. I don't think so. I'm sure it's part of it, but the other part which intrigues me is the Kira/Sisko conflicts. We don't have those on TNG. There's no conflict between Picard and Number One.

Q: There was a great moment representing that in your episode when Sisko said to Kira, "You go over my head again, I'll serve yours on a silver platter."

A: I love that. That to me is more human, it is more contemporary--and I'm talking about 1993. Sometimes we have to work together with people with whom we occasionally disagree with and have differences of opinion with, yet despite that they are capable of fulfilling their job. In the pilot, I think Sisko said, "I want you because you're Bajoran." He could have had any one of a million Bajorans, somebody who would say, "Yes, sir, whatever you want." He wanted somebody who comes from the background of Kira, who was in the underground against the Cardassians. A nationalist, so to speak. It intrigues me because I feel that, yes, we are changing, but we are not necessarily becoming more advanced. There's nationalism 2,000 years from now and it will always be there because it's something genetically inside us. Like racism, which is something that's always coming out. We only seemingly live in a better social society if we are able to combat it, but the moment we let our guard down, bingo, there's the conflict. I like that in DS9 when it comes down to the Kira/Sisko conflict. It's politics, but it's the politics of Starfleet, of the larger unit which says "We want to expand our influence," and the smaller unit which is the planet Bajor which says, "Hey, it's all very nice but you're taking over. We don't want you either." Talking about metaphors. The Americans in Somalia. Who's interest are we really representing?

Q: But the allegory makes it more powerful for the viewing audience.

A: A critic might say, "If you're doing this, it's basically propaganda for a certain philosophy," which it probably is although I'm not sure whether episodic television can seriously be accused of that one. It's just too short, too superficial. Occasionally you hit a nerve, but most of the time these allegories are just pointing out something, but I would not say they are going to reform the world.

Q: What are you feelings regarding this new ensemble of characters?

A: There's something intriguing about Odo, and part of is that I'm doing a show right now which features Odo. He is trying to discover where he came from but he unfortunately winds up with somebody he doesn't believe. He doesn't believe anybody to begin with, but this guy he *really* doesn't believe. When this guy suddenly begins to tune in on Odo's shape-shifting capability, he says, "Maybe I know something that might be intriguing to you." And then Odo's character says, "Forget it, you're a liar and a thief and I can't trust you," but then follows him anyway. It's intriguing, because there is a person who's very, very distrustful, which makes the perfect sheriff. He pushes the envelope of what the police should be. The police should be trusting nobody, and Odo's philosophy of arrest first, ask questions later is an intriguing aspect of his profession which obviously puts him into conflict with Sisko. I hope that we can put that beyond words and make it more interesting, but right now it's strictly, "I want to arrest him" and Sisko says, "You can't, you don't have any evidence." Those are the words. It's got to go beyond that. Again, we're talking about issues about society. We're talking about death penalty, the Napoleonic code versus the Anglo-Saxon code. Are we guilty until proven innocent or innocent until proven guilty? That is something intriguing, and Rene Auberjonois is such a fascinating actor.

Dax I haven't really explored yet. At this particular point she hasn't been big enough in the shows I've done to warrant any major exploration. Kira we talked about. Bashir is intriguing, although sometimes I'm afraid we're playing him a little bit too much for the buffoon.

Q: In "Past Prologue" he certainly seemed that way.

A: That bothers me a little bit. There's got to be something else; another way to handle him. O'Brien is similar to Dax as far as my shows because he's in the background. With Avery in the traditional command position, we're going in a different way now. We're suddenly beginning to say, "Hey, wait a moment, we do make mistakes and we do have problems with each other. We don't all run around with a valium-spiked brain that says, 'Everything is going to work out just fine.'"

Q: The old STAR TREK certainly did not do that.

A: No, that was the development of TNG, that we are so advanced. I think that was Gene's major input. Now we're talking about a new generation of creators, Berman and Piller who have a different outlook on man. Which is fine. You don't want DS9 to be the same as TNG except that the damn thing floats around in orbit. That would be boring and non-creative.

Q: But the old STAR TREK had the optimism that mankind is going to be okay, yet Kirk, Spock and McCoy could get into each other's face and it didn't matter. In TNG we get the same message that everything is going to be okay, yet everybody gets along like they're on valium or something.

A: Right, but it seems to work.

Q: Do you find this setting limiting?

A: Not really. Let's face it, if this was a German show I would say yes, but this is an American show. It is GUNSMOKE, it's the town that everybody comes to. Get the characters in there. That's actually the selling point and because of its setting it will become more of a character show. We get the people in there who represent the different opinions. We don't have to schlep through some deserted canyon in order to get there, they have to come to us.

Q: Certainly someone like Andrew Robinson as Garick was a very good character.

A: Yes, and I hope he'll be back. You don't know what to make of him and neither did the actor in the beginning. That is intriguing for everyone who comes on the show, unless it's somebody who has watched the show and studied it. But an actor who is suddenly thrown into a particular make-up, which way do you go? You can go any way you want.

Q: Do you think cross-overs from NEXT GEN is intriguing or a contrived means of story development?

A: We have established in the pilot that there is a connection between the two series. I don't think the writers will bring people in just because they were successful on the other show. There's got to be a modus operandi to bring them in. As long as it doesn't become a crutch it should work.

Q: Could you summarize what an audience coming into STAR TREK for the first time via DEEP SPACE NINE could expect?

A: As we've been talking about, I think it's the internal conflict between the people. Anybody who saw the pilot and read the article by Rick Berman and Michael Piller in TV GUIDE, has to be aware of the fact that we had an unwilling leader of the group in Sisko. Now *that* is intriguing. If he was unwilling once, even though at the end he said he's going to fulfill his obligations, there is a time bomb in that character. He's not the character anymore who says, "I'm loyalty above all and I'm going down with the ship." There is a possibility that he might do something totally different, totally unexpected. There is a conflict within Sisko and there are conflicts within Kira, is she loyal to Starfleet, is she loyal to Bajor, can she be loyal to both of them? The same thing with

Odo, can he be loyal to Starfleet's existing code of law or his own? I'm sure with Dax you've got the conflict of who she is and who she's got inside her, and so on. There are internal conflicts, which is what real characters are made out of and from which tragedies happen, as well as comedy and drama. This is humanity at work. Then you have the conflicts between the various elements within the main group, plus you have the conflicts between the group that runs the station and the strangers who are coming in and want to pursue their own agendas. It seems to me, just looking at the two scripts that I did, there's got to be a lot more sparks than in TNG. And that's fun. I believe there will always be conflict, there will always be war. There will never be the point where we're all running around like we're on valium. We have to handle it. We have to do something. There will never be a time when we say, "Everything's been solved." The moment that happens, it's time to buy a bouquet, go to the next cemetery and wait until it's your turn.

An Interview With Paul Lynch

Paul Lynch, whose genre credits include BEAUTY AND THE BEAST and the recent revival of DARK SHADOWS, was an early directorial pioneer of THE NEXT GENERATION, having helmed season one's "The Naked Now." Since then he has taken the reigns of "11001001", "Unnatural Selection", "A Matter of Time" and "First Duty." Additionally, he is helming several episodes of DEEP SPACE NINE, including "A Man Alone" and "Babel."

Q: Well, we're certainly in a different environment than the one found on NEXT GENERATION.

A: It's truly intriguing and there's nothing on television these days that you really *don't* know where it's going. With this one, you never quite know.

Q: The "Encounter at Farpoint" pilot of NEXT GENERATION seemingly felt obligated to explore all the characters and provide as much information as it could in two hours. DEEP SPACE NINE, conversely, has taken a more leisurely pace. For instance, we really don't start to understand the relationship between Sisko and Dax until "A Man Alone."

A: The first few episodes of THE NEXT GENERATION it was the Starfleet people on the ship themselves. On this one they've got different types of people to explore, Bajorans, Ferengi and all sorts of things, right off the top. We can explore them because it's a space station. There are people from truly different environments, and you didn't really have that off the top of NEXT GENERATION because you had these set people on a ship. That's a big difference.

Q: Rick Kolbe's opinion is that the Deep Space Nine setting is very much like Dodge City; that this show, to a certain extent, has a lot in common with GUNSMOKE.

A: That's right. NEXT GENERATION is WAGON TRAIN and this is GUNSMOKE.

Q: The opening of "A Man Alone" was truly enjoyable, because you have Odo and Quark discussing the nature of male/female relationships, and it's hysterical.

A: And that keeps going, at least in the episodes that I've done. That kind of bit is a running piece of business they do between themselves about *everything*. Odo is always reacting against Quark and it's quite fun. It's a very interesting relationship they've set up between these two people, who obstensively hate each other but on the other hand would die for each other.

Q: What do you think of the difference in tone between the two series?

A: The one thing that strikes me is that this is funnier. Like the relationship between Quark and Odo. There's a general lightness to them that wasn't in the NEXT GENERATION. And the conflict between everyone on that station, because they're from different places and different worlds. Those are two differences, the third one being special effects and the creatures that you find on this space station.

Q: NEXT GENERATION has done a very good job in covering up the fact that there is such a lack of conflict between the characters, yet when you watch DEEP SPACE NINE you have to sort of smile and say, "Ah, this is what's been missing."

A: Yes, because it makes you realize it. There's conflict between Sisko and Kira; there's a running bit between Odo and Quark. And in later episodes a conflict grows between Sisko and Odo, and a conflict between Quark and Sisko. That keeps it on the edge a little bit. What I think the show genuinely consists of is a nice group of people with a good moral stance in truly interesting stories that you really haven't seen.